TELL ME YOU LOVE ME

TELL ME
YOU LOVE ME

A Sharecropper's Daughter Tells Her Story

LORETTA MILLER MEHL

TELL ME YOU LOVE ME
A SHARECROPPER'S DAUGHTER TELLS HER STORY

iUniverse books may be ordered through booksellers or by contacting:

iUniverse
1663 Liberty Drive
Bloomington, IN 47403
www.iuniverse.com
1-800-Authors (1-800-288-4677)

ISBN: 978-1-4917-7673-5 (sc)
ISBN: 978-1-4917-7675-9 (hc)
ISBN: 978-1-4917-7674-2 (e)

Library of Congress Control Number: 2015918635

Print information available on the last page.

iUniverse rev. date: 11/06/2015

Dedicated to my daughter, Sheri.
Thank you for encouraging me to write. I love you!

Table of Contents

Acknowledgements

Over twenty years ago, my daughter, Sheri, handed me a blank notebook and requested, "Write about your growing up years." Her encouragement and that of family and friends resulted in this book, a collection of stories from my life.

Many who read portions of my work provided helpful suggestions. I am especially appreciative for my writer's group in Eugene, Oregon, whose friendship and critique I deeply value. I also want to thank all those who responded to my many phone calls and questions to validate my memories, some of them regarding events as long ago as eighty years. As much as possible, I've tried to stay true to recollections of my life.

At age eighty-eight, several persons who could "set me straight" have passed on. I recognize my life has been influenced and shaped by their love and strong character traits of honesty, strength, hard work, faith and hope. Many of the people I've written about faced impossible odds, never having the opportunity for an adequate education.

Although I struggled growing up in poverty, my family did what they thought to be honest and right and I acknowledge that it is their strength of character and actions of love that provide me the opportunity to share my story.

I'm thankful for all who reviewed individual chapters and made suggestions and asked for clarifications. Their willingness to assist me in this grand project is greatly treasured.

Introduction

These stories were written over a period of thirty plus years. The book opens with me as a child, a sharecropper's daughter, standing in a vegetable garden, listening to my father sing "Amazing Grace" in the distance as he plows the fields barefoot.

Like many who grew up in the South during the Great Depression, these narratives tell of my experience with poverty and of people who worked relentlessly to keep their families intact though hard work and great personal sacrifice. I grew up surrounded by a community who sought to abide by a strict moral code and relied upon God to live out their Christian faith. My father saved every penny to buy his farm in Arkansas, located about sixty miles northwest of Little Rock. He never borrowed money; he saved for every purchase. We did without until he could pay cash.

My earliest memories include living in a two-room sharecropper's shack. One room called "the living room" was where we all slept; the other room, the kitchen, was used for cooking and eating. These stories are a record of many of the experiences of our family and the farming community where I grew up. I've tried to provide windows into the past for all those interested in the American experience and for those who may have ancestors who lived under similar circumstances, but who never heard this perspective.

By sharing my life, I hope those who read may be encouraged to express their love vocally and be inspired to write their unique family history. At my age, I desire my children and relatives know this portion of their family history and understand the providence of the Lord that has placed them where they are today. The written words are a part of my legacy and one thing I've learned, "It's not only how you live, but what you say that counts."

Loretta Miller Mehl
Eugene, Oregon
August 2015

www.LorettaMillerMehl.com

THE WORDS I LONGED TO HEAR

M y husband and I have been following the paved road for several miles when we come to the dirt road that leads to the farm. As I've done many times, I'm returning to the place of my childhood. Looking across the fields lined by trees, my thoughts transport me back to the days I walked along this same road to catch the school bus every weekday, and early mornings when I walked over the hill to the small white church for Sunday school and church. Early memories, which I always carry with me, surface as we drive.

As a young child, during a hot spring morning, I hear my father singing "Amazing Grace" in the distance. The words echo throughout our narrow valley. My father, Arthur Daniel Miller, wears patched overalls of denim and a faded, torn work shirt. He walks barefoot in the freshly-turned ground following the plow pulled by the team of horses.

I know the words and I sing along with Daddy.

Amazing grace! How sweet the sound
That saved a wretch like me!
I once was lost, but now am found,
Was blind, but now I see.

We often sing the song in church that speaks of the amazing grace of Jesus' love. I ponder the meaning of the words. I do not believe Daddy and I are wretches, but I'm not sure what the word means. I've heard of people being lost, but I've never been. When I go with my sister or brother to search for wild flowers in the woods, we stay near the paths and have no trouble finding our way home. I close my eyes to imagine being blind, but quickly open them to look at the sunlight shining on the green meadow below the barnyard.

Standing in our vegetable garden, I remove weeds from around young tomato plants. I'm wearing a floppy sunbonnet on my head, which my mother insists I need to protect my face and neck. "Keep your skin nice and white; don't want you going around lookin' like an Indian." Every time she tells me this I think, "What a funny remark," for I've heard we have an Indian ancestor several generations back.

My short cotton dress leaves my arms and legs exposed to the attack of the sweat bees. I'm barefoot and the soil burns hot on my feet. My mother brings me cold water, freshly drawn from the well. She stays to pick the small green lettuce leaves and pull some tender new onions from the carefully tended rows.

My father spends every daylight hour trying to make the farm produce enough food for his family and a cash crop. He stops at noon just long enough to eat and then rushes back for more work that will continue until it's too dark to see. Upon arriving back at the house, he lights the coal-oil lantern and makes his way to the barn to milk the cows and feed the pigs. After supper, often cold cornbread crumbled in milk, and eaten with a slice of ham, he falls into bed exhausted.

In the springtime, hope returns that the coming year will be better than in years past. Our family dreams of a bountiful harvest, but often the dreams are unrealized because of drought, flood, or the boll weevil. Daddy seems preoccupied by the struggle to beat out an existence from the unyielding land. I think he may be afraid of the future.

In the distance I hear him singing of the amazing grace and love of Jesus, but I wonder if my father loves me. He has never told me so. He never shows any expressions of love toward me, although he quickly tells me if I displease him. "You kids keep working. Can't expect cotton to grow all choked by weeds. Never seen such lazy kids in my life!"

My father's cross words upset me and his handsome, lean face seldom smiles. He pushes himself to the limit and he expects his children to doggedly work as he has always done.

The lack of money causes many arguments between Mama and Daddy. She wants nice things for her children, and he appears determined to save every penny as a protection against poverty. I try not to ask for money, but necessity forces me. "I'm not made of money," he flings at me with the nickel I need for a pencil.

My mother begs my father to kiss and hug her, but he makes a face and pushes her away. She gets very quiet and a hurt look fills her dark brown eyes. Instead, he pretends to kiss all the pretty young cousins who come to visit.

Time and distance have removed the Arkansas farm and its people that were a vital part of my life. As we drive the country roads I recall the pain of my childhood. Looking back I realize now how much I needed my father's approval.

My father's reluctance to show affection appeared to be the trait I witnessed in Daddy's mother, my grandmother. Her lack of emotions seemed held down, buried. I never saw her lose her temper. I never heard her laugh or cry. Had she locked away all emotion to survive after my grandfather took his own life, leaving her with seven young children?

As we drive, I look for long-forgotten landmarks: the stream where I caught crawfish and tiny minnows, the large oak tree located in the middle of the country road. As we climb the hill, the farmhouse comes into view. My husband blows the horn at my request, and Mama and Daddy hurry from the house to greet us. Mama and I cry as we hug one another and Daddy lets me embrace him and kiss his cheek. He holds himself slightly away and does not hug me back. Mama enfolds me tightly, kissing me over and over. Her first daughter, the little girl she adored, has returned home to visit.

Mama tends the garden, cans the produce, scrubs the floors, and bakes pies and cakes. She prepares three meals each day. Mama starts breakfast with a menu unchanged since my childhood: eggs, bacon, hot biscuits served with homemade jam and thick milk gravy. My mother has grown heavy from childbearing and eating the rich diet, but she is still pretty, her face framed by abundant white hair. Daddy remains lean and trim. His thick dark hair has disappeared leaving a bald head edged in gray. The weathered face shows surprisingly few wrinkles, a mouth firm and piercing blue eyes.

On the second day my father seeks me out. "Thought I'd take you by the graveyard to see your grandmother's grave." He appears pleased that I will go with him. He puts a hoe in the back of the truck to clear the grave of weeds and carries a small bouquet of artificial flowers to place near her tombstone.

"I miss her so much," he tells me as he works on the grave. "My sister Faye made a terrible remark at Ma's funeral. She said, 'Perhaps Arthur did love Mother after all.'" His voice shakes with emotion. "I did more for Ma than all the other kids put together. I got the Old-Age Pension for her. Found out about it, went over and took her in the truck to sign up. I bought her house shoes and sweaters to keep her warm; brought her home with me whenever she wanted to come. I was good to Ma! No one can deny it! Imagine Faye saying a thing like that!"

It was a long speech for an unusually silent man. Slow tears started down the weather-beaten cheeks. He brushed them away with the back of his hand. I doubt my father had ever told his mother how dearly he loved her during her long life, nor do I think he will ever say he loves me.

How I wish that he could say the words, while he's alive to say them, and I'm alive to hear them.

I reach out my hand to touch his shoulder. "I understand. I know that you loved Grandma and I think that she knew it, too." My voice comes out in a near sob and hot tears sting my eyes. I go to him and hold him tightly in my arms. "I love you, Daddy," I tell him as gently as a mother trying to comfort her small son, but he does not respond.

FROM THIS DAY FORWARD

On Christmas Day, 1924, my parents, Arthur Daniel Miller and Jewell Gertrude Chandler began a marriage "For richer or poorer, For better or worse, In sickness and in health, Till death do us part" that lasted for 71 years. The road ahead was not an easy one. My mother, barely 19 years old and my father not yet 21, started with no house, no job, no money, and little education.

Daddy brought his bride to his mother's house in Caney Valley. Later they moved into a sharecropper's shack on great uncle Forrest Griswood's farm. I remember this place as my first home, an unpainted two-room shack with broken windows covered by cardboard. When rains came, the roof leaked. We ran to put pots and pans underneath the steady drips of water to protect our beds. Newspapers pasted on the inside walls for insulation did little to keep the house warm. Nothing kept out the cold, for the wind penetrated the cracks around windows, doors, and wooden siding.

Our house contained two beds with iron bedsteads that held fluffy, soft mattresses called feather beds, passed down in the family. Hand-made quilts, sheets and pillowcases were made from feed sacks. Furnishings included four unpainted straight-back chairs, a beat-up wooden table and an old wood-burning stove.

We drew water from our well with a bucket tied to rope. We harvested vegetables from the garden. Butchered hogs provided meat; chickens produced eggs and poultry; a couple of cows furnished milk and butter. Mama's father gave her a cow and chickens as a wedding gift. Daddy purchased the absolute necessities of flour, sugar, salt, coffee, baking powder and baking soda.

I have only one baby picture of me. Another was taken with my family when I was two years old. I'm dressed in a pretty coat and matching hat, a gift from relatives in Little Rock. Our family looks surprisingly well clothed. Daddy wore a suit with a tie; Mama, a stylish dress and a fancy hat. My baby sister's wrap and cap look new. My brother Hershel wore coveralls. In the original, tiny snapshot torn at the corner and aged to sepia tone, I catch a glimpse of myself as a child with chubby cheeks and fat little legs. You might never guess from the picture that we lived in poverty, or that all of my family went barefoot in the summer to save our shoes for church.

Mama bore three children in less than five years: Hershel Daniel, the eldest; me, Loretta Gertrude nicknamed Rita; and my sister, Opal Mae. Then eight years later, Lewis Earl was born. For years I thought Mama was attended at home by a midwife. Mama told Lewis, "an elderly colored woman assisted your birth." When I questioned my father years later, he said a doctor delivered each of us. To my knowledge Mama never had a medical examination for pre-natal care for the three older children.

Several years after Lewis' birth, Mama suffered a miscarriage. I had no idea why she "took to her bed" looking pale and drawn, and unable to do the household chores. No one explained to me what happened. She never spoke of losing the baby, nor did she ever mention a similar occurrence when we worked as sharecroppers. My cousin Ellen said our families were working in the bottomland when my mother became ill and started to walk home. They heard her screaming for help and when they ran to her "there was blood everywhere."

I doubt that Daddy and Mama had visions of wealth: the daily demand for food and shelter was their all-consuming concern. Our family, ill clothed and poorly housed, ate whatever food was available. My parents rarely complained. Money became an obsession, a protection against extreme want, so Daddy saved every penny.

Finally as the country climbed from the depths of the Depression, cotton and corn brought more money on the local market. The few pennies saved became nickels and dimes, and finally, dollars. Daddy's question, "When can I buy my own farm?" seemed uttermost in his thoughts.

The prosperous men owned farms. Mama's father, George Washington Chandler, and his wife, Charity, bought a farm in the Hill Creek community in 1902. Mama was born there in 1905 and lived in the same house until she and Daddy married. She was one of the ten heirs to inherit a portion of the farm when Grandpa Chandler died. Daddy bought the Chandler farm parcel by parcel from Mama's siblings.

At last Daddy realized his dream, even though he had purchased a farm that was far from prosperous. The soil, depleted by row crops, grew dense weeds, gullies cut across the fields, and hedgerows of tangled brush flourished. Daddy worked from the break of day until nightfall and he could no longer see the work site. He committed his life to making the farm produce enough money to "get ahead."

Until eleven years of age, I lived as a sharecropper's daughter, first on great uncle Forrest's place, and then in a little house on the Chandler farm. When Daddy bought the property, we moved to the owner's residence. Though larger, it had no modern conveniences, electricity or running water. My life barely changed.

Although my brothers and sister seemed to accept our

marginal existence, I struggled with the negative aspects of poverty. The shabby furnishings, dresses of cheap material, and an outhouse for a toilet embarrassed me. My father's relentless obsession with money appeared to intensify. Six years later, at age seventeen, I left the farm forever.

Paid In Full

I was born in an obscure community called Hill Creek, named for the two main features of the land. My birthplace was definitely not the center of the universe: culturally, politically, educationally, or any other category that would distinguish it from countless other places in the rural area of Arkansas. At the time of my birth in 1927, everyone was suffering from "times being so hard up," we might as well have already been in the Great Depression years. Money was considered a rare possession and that became the focus of my father's life.

During the summer of 1993 my husband and I drove from Oregon to Arkansas to visit my elderly parents. My father was almost 90 years old and he and my mother were living on the farm where my mother had been born, and where I had been born. At my request, my husband, Bill, had been recording my Mom and Dad as I interviewed them about my family history. He had finished taping the video and turned off the camera and almost missed what turned out to be perhaps the most interesting part of the discussion.

Knowing that many births in the rural areas had been attended by a black midwife, I asked my dad, "Tell me, Daddy, did you have a midwife when we children were born?"

"No, we did not," Daddy responded. "We sent to town to get the doctor to come." His old eyes lighted up as he was remembering. "I'll never forget the night your brother Hershel was born. It was

December and the weather had been awfully cold. It had been raining for several days and the dirt road was "knee-deep" in mud. Well, Dr. Goatcher drove out in his Model T Ford, one of the first cars in the area. He got stuck down yonder below the hill. He had to walk the rest of the way up to the farm house in the pourin' rain. Got here just in time to deliver your brother."

"Oh, my," I exclaimed. "After having such a difficult time getting here through all that mud and rain, do you remember what he charged?"

"Yep, I certainly do!" Daddy replied. "He charged me five dollars. And it was hard to pay that much during them hard times!"

I wanted to hear more. This was fascinating information that I had never before heard. "Well," I continued, "That was two years before I was born. So what did you have to pay when I came along?"

There was a twinkle in Daddy's eyes as he said, "By that time the price had really gone way up! An' I had to pay a lot more! The doctor charged twice as much and you cost $10.00!"

As I sat pondering just how much things had changed since 1927, I remembered that in the year 1983 when my granddaughter, Elisabeth, was born by C-section, the cost for the hospital stay alone, for a period of 5 days and without further complications, was over $10,000.

Epilogue

My father's memory usually appeared quite accurate during his old age. I was therefore very surprised when I checked my birth certificate and found the name of the doctor who had signed was Dr. Kelso, and not Dr. Goatcher, as my father had told me.

SHARECROPPER'S CHILD

The circumstances of my birth as a sharecropper's child placed me in poverty that touched all aspects of my life. Hard work was a large part of our existence and children were expected to do whatever they could to help. In addition to work in the fields, begun in the springtime and lasting through the fall, we performed everyday chores throughout the year.

During my sharecropper years, we used a bucket tied to the end of a rope to draw water from the well. Later, Daddy installed a hand-operated pump. Whenever possible, a barrel placed beneath the eaves of the tin roof of our house caught rainwater to use for the washing of clothing and hair. The well water had such high mineral content that it discolored clothing and utensils with rust colored stains. In contrast, the rainwater was so pure it left the clothing white and our hair soft and shiny.

Once we brought a notice home from school that someone in our class had "cooties" and a nurse from the Health Department examined each child. As she checked my thick hair she said to me, "For goodness sakes, don't ever let cooties get started in this head of hair!" My hair was so thick she probably thought eradicating the bugs would be an impossible task.

We could never bathe often and this was a source of embarrassment for me. The time-consuming process involved drawing water from the well, carrying large buckets full into the house, building a fire to heat our bath water, and trying to find the privacy to bathe. We resorted to "spit baths" using a cloth and a wash pan with an occasional bath in the wash tub or the creek.

Washing clothes was an even bigger chore. We heated water in the large wash pot located in the yard and scrubbed the clothing by hand on a washboard. Mama allowed extra time for boiling the white clothes in the wash pot to get them snowy clean. The job required a large amount of water to wash and then rinse everything before hanging the laundry on the clothesline. In the summertime the clothes dried in the hot sunshine and soft breezes, leaving a delightful fresh scent. In freezing weather the clothes froze stiff as boards and we took the laundry inside and hung on improvised clotheslines stretched across the living room ceiling. Mama's hands broke open in the wintertime, sore and red from working in the cold.

Mama used lye soap she made for doing the laundry. She saved fat rendered from the skin and scraps of butchered hogs for soap-making day. To save a few pennies, my friend's family made their own lye by a slow-drip process through a hollow log using wood-ashes, The procedure required time and effort, so Daddy bought a can of lye at the store to speed up the process.

We stood over the black wash pot and stirred for what seemed like hours during the cooking process. Later, when the concoction was allowed to cool, it became a firm mass that Mama cut into bars. The off-white soap, although very hard on the hands, worked quite well at cleaning the ground-in dirt from overalls and long-handled underwear soiled from grime, mud, and manure.

Many pieces of the laundry needed ironing each week. Temperatures of flatirons heated in the fireplace or on top of the cook stove were difficult to adjust. If the iron got too hot, I scorched the item. Mama warned, "Please be careful not to burn the clothing. When your daddy and I were first married he decided to press the vest of his new suit. The iron was so hot that it burned a hole right through the material."

We starched and then ironed the washed items to perfection. We made our own starch by cooking flour and water and then thinning it to the right consistency. We dipped dresses, shirts, table clothes and dresser scarves into the mixture one by one, squeezed as dry as possible and then hung them out to dry again. Later we dampened the starched items with water from a bottle fitted with a small sprinkling attachment, rolled items into small wads and wrapped them in a towel to await ironing.

After spending long days working in the fields, we children helped with the chores at the barn and in the house. We took turns carrying heavy loads of wood to burn in the cook stove and the fireplace. We drew water from the well with the help of a pulley and carried big metal buckets, one held in each hand, for use inside the house. We scrubbed the bare wooden floors and dusted the furniture. We washed and dried dishes by hand.

Each of the children in our family worked in the cotton fields as soon as we were capable of holding a hoe or picking a lock of cotton.

I never learned to do two things: how to milk the cows or plow the fields. I tried very hard to learn both. I did not have strength in my hands and wrists to milk properly. Daddy thought I purposely would not learn, but that was not true.

Years later, when my older brother Hershel was away during World War II, Daddy desperately needed help with the farm work and decided that I should learn to plow the fields. After hitching up the mule and telling me what to do, he left me to plow between the furrows. The mule had other ideas. Although I tugged and pulled with all my strength, I could not get the mule to go where

I was supposed to plow. Finally the mule started for the barn pulling the plow with me hanging on desperately behind. I was crying in frustration and completely defeated. My father never again asked me to plow the fields.

SPECIAL AND LOVED

The name on her birth certificate was much shorter than Audrey Opal Mae Belle Spier, but she used the longer version to impress people. She displayed a unique vitality and enjoyment of life that made me want to be like her.

I do not remember the first time I met my cousin Audrey; she was always a part of my life. When our family lived in the sharecropper's house, we walked several miles over the hill to visit her family. Earliest memories of her home included her mother, Aunt Altie, and husband, Uncle Will. She had two older brothers, Bob and Clarence. They lived in a small, weather-beaten house with a white picket fence covered with vines of roses. Clusters of the flowers covered an archway over the gate.

Mama and Daddy walked with the three small children when we visited Audrey and her family; my infant sister, me, two years old, and my brother, almost four. Daddy carried the baby, but I was "the big girl who could walk."

I always liked going to Aunt Altie's house, for Audrey made me feel special. Several years older, she carted me around on her hip, and focused attention on me. Wedged in birth order between my big brother and my baby sister, I longed to feel important.

When I was three years old, my aunt asked permission to keep me for a week. I was too young to remember many details about the visit. I do recall Audrey and my aunt weeded the vegetable garden before deciding they were thirsty. I followed them to the well located on a small back porch. Audrey let down the bucket and drew up the icy cold water. "Ah," Aunt Altie said, "Doesn't this water taste great?" After we drank our fill from the tin dipper, the precious remainder was deposited in a wooden bucket kept on a high shelf. Every drop was conserved to water plants, cook or wash. My aunt taught me to appreciate the blessing of water on a hot, humid day.

I ventured into the yard one day picking up small stones. An old rooster suddenly attacked me with a flying leap. I was terribly frightened and screamed. Audrey ran outside and picked me up. I hated that rooster and decided to never go outside by myself again.

On another visit when Audrey was a teenager, she decided to see how I would look wearing her cosmetics. She emphasized my dark brows and eyelashes, put eye shadow above my blue eyes, and painted my high cheek bones with rouge. She finished by adding bright red lipstick. I was amazed at the transformation as I peered into the high mirror over the tall chest of drawers.

When I was nearing the teen years, an incident happened that increased my shyness. Several people were gathered at Aunt Altie's house—both adults and children. We watched Audrey practicing gymnastics in the back yard. She flipped over and over, doing beautiful handsprings without effort, always coming to a stop standing gracefully. I wanted desperately to perform a handspring, but was afraid I might fail. I slipped away to the front yard to practice, but fell in a disgraceful heap and heard sudden laughter. I had not fooled Audrey. She guessed what I planned and followed me around the side of the house. Terribly embarrassed, I felt my cheeks flaming. I would never attempt to do handsprings again, ever. Strangely, I did not feel angry with her.

Audrey and her brother Bob were the first people I knew to own a Victrola. They tried out various dance steps to the tunes:

Constantinople, When the Moon Comes over the Mountain, K-K-Katy—You're the Only Girl that I Adore. My cousin never attended dances, which were usually held at roadhouses, dance halls or bars. Nice girls did not go where alcoholic drinks were served.

Audrey played on a girls' basketball team at school. She received blue shorts and a white shirt for her uniform. One day she came home with a note that requested the shorts should be hemmed up three inches. Her stepfather voiced his displeasure. "No daughter of mine," and he did consider her his very own, "is going to expose herself in public wearing such garb!" Some kind of compromise was reached, for Audrey continued to play through junior high and excelled in the sport.

When she was younger, the school term had been cut to four months because of lack of funds. Divided into low and high sessions, each grade often took two years to complete. Those who paid tuition went for the full term. But Aunt Altie's family could not afford to pay. Audrey was a young lady by the time she finished Springfield Junior High and did not continue her education at Morrilton High School.

Audrey once talked to me about the father she never knew—an educated man who taught school. He died of a gunshot wound after an argument with his brother. She was told her father's last words were "See that the kids get a good education." The circumstances that took his life made his final instructions impossible because of lack of money.

Audrey was a popular young woman, the life of any gathering. She loved to sing and accompanied herself on the guitar. She started dating in junior high school and G.F. became her faithful boyfriend. He drove an old Model T Ford. Our cousin Odusca loved to tease Audrey by singing, "I'll be down to get you in a Model T, Baby!"

G.F. was a handsome, personable young man, both steady and dependable. Everyone thought he would be a fine husband and the years proved them right.

Audrey was always one of my favorite people, for she made me feel special and loved. Returning home from high school one day while she visited with my mother in the kitchen, I heard my name mentioned. "I think Rita is really lovely when she wears the aqua-colored dress that matches her eyes," she said. "What fantastically beautiful eyes she has!" I never knew anyone thought my eyes beautiful. I told no one about the overheard conversation which I treasured then, and still do.

Forty years later my husband took a picture of Audrey and G.F., still an attractive couple, sitting on the porch swing at my parents' house. Grandparents at the time, Audrey had stylish snow-white hair, while G.F. had changed little. They had one son, Jerry Robert, and two granddaughters.

Audrey, in her eighties, maintains her spotless picturesque house. Her husband requires extra care since he suffered a stroke. I call her from time to time. We were chatting one day when she astonished me by exclaiming, "I wish I could have been more like you—kind and good!" She joyfully voices her affection for me as she repeats the words I've heard from her since childhood, "I love you."

YOU NEVER CAN TELL

A horse-drawn wagon stopped in front of our small, sharecropper's house. High up front, in a wooden spring seat, an old gray-haired black woman looked down at my father and me. As we walked toward the wagon, my father leading me by the hand, the woman smiled warmly.

"Hi, Aunt Julie," was my father's affectionate greeting. "Got a little girl here that needs some warts taken off."

"That so? Be glad to do it," Aunt Julie replied with self-assurance.

Daddy lifted me up to sit beside the elderly woman. "Would you like to sell your warts to me?" she asked.

When I nodded, she reached out and took my small white hands in her large, wrinkled brown ones. Very carefully she counted my warts, "One, two, three, four, five. Lawsy me, chile," she said, "You been playin' with toad frogs?"

"Well, yes, I have," I admitted. She reached into her clothing and took some pennies out of a pocket. Carefully, one by one, she counted the pennies, as she placed them in my palm. "One for each wart," she said as she rubbed each wart carefully, then turned aside to mutter sounds scarcely audible.

She turned back to me and smiled, "Forget about your warts, honey chile, cause they'll soon be gone."

Daddy had been standing nearby. When Aunt Julie indicated that she had finished, he came over and lifted me down from the wagon.

"Much obliged to you, Aunt Julie," he said, as he placed some coins in her hand. "Appreciate you stopping by and helpin' us out."

"Glad to do it, jest call on me anytime," and with a "giddy-up" to her horse and a slap with the reins, the woman pulled away, driving slowly down the dirt road.

"Forget all about the warts," Daddy said. "Just like Aunt Julie told you."

I couldn't help checking my warts when I was busy washing dishes or helping pull weeds, but they didn't look any different from what they ever had.

"Can Aunt Julie really take my warts off?" I asked Daddy.

"Folks say she sure can. Never fails. Has done it many, many times. You just be patient, it may take a while," Daddy reassured me.

"Daddy, Aunt Julie said something I couldn't hear. Do you know what it was?"

"No, no one knows. I heard she can't tell, for if she does, she might lose the power to make the warts go away."

We kids were always getting warts on our hands and Mama kept warning us, "Playin' with toad frogs is a sure-fire way to catch warts, especially if you let the toads wee-wee on your hands!" and they often did.

"Quick, better wash your hands!" Mama would exclaim.

The baby toads appeared mysteriously after the warm spring rains. Soon as the sun went down they hopped all over the yard. My sister and I used them to play pranks on our mother, just like our playmates did on us. "Hold out your hand," my sister said while placing a tiny toad in the outstretched palm. The toad leaped and we squealed and Mama acted surprised. "Oh, you awful kids, you," she'd say. But we knew she really didn't think we were awful. We played the same trick with grasshoppers and she always acted as if she was expecting something special. We didn't like the grasshoppers very well though, for they were always "gettin' even" by spitting tobacco juice on us, at least that's what we called it.

I had lots of things to do besides playing, for I stayed busy helping Mama and my sister in the garden. I hoed the vegetables to remove weeds, picked peas in their glossy pods, and searched for cucumbers in the thick green vines.

That was just a few of many jobs. We never seemed to finish drawing water from the well. We kept the trough full so the cows and horses had plenty to drink when they came to the barn. We carried water to fill the reservoir in the kitchen stove to have hot water for cooking, canning, washing dishes and bathing.

At the end of the day the chickens needed feeding, eggs gathered, and wood brought in for the cook stove. We had little time to play during the summertime days. But when chores were finished, during the long period of twilight before darkness fell, we played all we wanted; hop-scotch, kick-the-can, red rover red rover, and farmer in the dell. We stopped to chase the lightning bugs flashing their little lanterns, or gathered up the small toads hopping around under foot.

As I went about my work I'd sometimes glance at my warts, thinking that Aunt Julie's cure wasn't working this time. The warts looked the same size—no bigger or smaller, and I always counted, hoping that at least one of them might be gone, but they were all there.

"Sure wish these warts would go away," I told my sister, Opal. "What a nuisance, they're always getting in my way."

By that time of the year we finished "choppin' cotton" and the corn was "laid by." We had time to play with the neighbor kids, and walked up Rocky Hollow creek to pick wild flowers.

The church homecoming was scheduled for the first Sunday

in June, and everyone looked forward to that day. "First Sunday in June Singing and Dinner on the Ground"—that's what we called it, although the dinner was not really on the ground.

The men carried out the church benches and improvised tables on which to place the food. The women spread tablecloths and then put out rows and rows of delicious food: huge platters of fried chicken, bowls of chicken and dumplings, chicken with cornbread dressing, country ham, spare ribs, and fresh-picked vegetables from the garden. For dessert we had every kind of pie and cake one might want: apple, peach, blackberry, coconut cream, chocolate, banana, and pecan. We stuffed ourselves until we couldn't eat one more bite.

The food and day of singing were equally anticipated and enjoyed. We all loved to sing, from the smallest kids to the old grandparents. Everyone sang with untiring enthusiasm. The day was a real celebration of praising the Lord in song. Singing groups came from churches at Overcup, Bald Knob, Center Ridge and Caney Valley. We had special music performed by duets, trios, and quartets, with numbers by our own Norwood Sisters.

Little kids sat on the front pews. When a child indicated he was brave enough to lead a song, Mr. Marvin Stover, the singing school teacher, announced the name. The entire congregation clapped and clapped after the number.

I'd see everyone I knew and felt fortunate to have a brand-new dress to wear. The day finally arrived and I donned my Sears Roebuck catalog dress, a light blue taffeta worn with new white shoes. I stood in front of the mirror to admire my new outfit and suddenly I looked down at my hands.

"Mama, Mama, guess what?" I couldn't believe my eyes.

She came running, "What's wrong, Rita? Is something the matter?"

"No, no. I'm fine, but look at my hands! The warts! They're all gone!" I held my hands up to examine them closely. They were perfectly smooth with not even a hint of a spot where the warts had been.

"Oh, Rita, that's great. I'm so glad they're gone." Mama gave me a hug. "Aunt Julie was right. Soon as you forgot about them, they went away."

"Wish I knew how she did it," I said, determined someday to try my luck at curing warts. I'd practice rubbing and counting carefully just like Aunt Julie, and I'd pay a penny for each one I hoped to remove. You never can tell, if someone thought I could take warts off, I just might be able to do it.

A Powerful Remedy

During one hot summer day, my three-year-old sister, Opal, and I stayed in the shade of the tall trees at the end of the cotton rows while Daddy and Mama worked. We often entertained ourselves. For the first hour we played in the dirt nearby, sweeping the area with a broken tree limb to clear a space.

"Let's make playhouses," I said. We drew an outline of a house in the dirt using a stick. Working with small rocks and seed pods, we divided the area into rooms. We furnished our house by using pieces of bark for beds and chairs and smooth flat stones for a table and stove. We marked pathways leading to the house with small pebbles we found nearby. We broke off small twigs from green bushes and stuck them upright for trees.

After exhausting the playhouse idea, we glanced around for other entertainment.

"Oh, look," I said. "There are lots of big leaves under the shade trees. Let's pick some and make crowns to wear on our heads." We collected an armful and then gathered small thorns from a nearby bush.

"Here, let me show you how to put them together," I said. I helped my sister fasten the plentiful leaves in a chain, making crowns. We went back to gather more to use for bracelets and belts. We kept busy and didn't bother our parents while they worked.

Eventually, they stopped at the end of the rows to get a drink of water from the glass jar wrapped in wet burlap. "What have you kids been doing?" Mama asked, as her eyes focused on the leaves being worn on our heads, waists, and wrists.

"Oh, no"! She gasped, "You kids picked poison ivy!" She hurriedly rinsed our hands, arms, legs and feet with water left in the drinking jar. Opal and I did not know about poison ivy. We wondered why such a fuss was being made.

I did not get one single spot from my encounter, not then, or in the coming years of walking through pastures and fields. Opal had fair skin and she was soon covered with itchy rash. Mama solved the problem. She used no fancy ointments or expensive trips to the doctor for the fast healing. Instead she applied one of Grandmother Charity Chandler's remedies that were passed on to my mother.

Fastidious people rejected the advice and suffered repeatedly from the itching and scratching. My second cousin Janice was eight years old when she broke out with poison ivy and had the worst case we ever saw. The more she itched, the more it spread, until her hands, legs and feet were covered with ugly sores. The more visits to the doctor and prescriptions from the drug store, the worse it spread. Finally, she could hardly walk. She suffered agony with itching from the oozing scabs.

Janice and I played together, but not since the inflammation had gotten so bad. She was spending most of her time in bed.

"Mama, you better tell Aunt Katherine how to cure the poison ivy," I pleaded.

"Now, Rita, you know as well as I do, she would never allow Janice to doctor herself." Mama shrugged.

But one day when we went to visit, Aunt Katherine was making apple pies and we were alone with Janice.

"Janice," Mama said," I know something that might cure your poison ivy."

"You do?" Janice exclaimed. "I'm willing to try anything. This stuff is driving me crazy!"

"Better not tell your mother. She'd probably have a fit!"

"Mama won't like it? Why? What's so bad about it?"

"You've heard country people use home remedies, like tea from blackberry roots to cure diarrhea?"

Janice nodded her head.

"My mother used a home remedy for curing poison ivy. Every time you go to the bathroom to wee-wee, put some on all the sore places on your legs and feet, arms, and every place you're itchin'. I'll bet in a short time you'll see a big improvement, and then you should heal completely."

"Honest, Cousin Jewell?" Janice looked appalled, not sure whether to believe what she had heard. "Seems like an awful thing to try! Mama makes me wash my hands all the time and I can't even play in the mud!"

"I know," my mother nodded, "but you need help bad."

"That's for sure," Janice agreed. "And I won't tell Mama. She wouldn't like it at all."

We didn't see Janice for over a week, but Aunt Lodus was talking about her when visiting one day. "Janice is finally getting over the poison ivy. What a bad time she's had. Never seen such a bad case. Aunt Katherine almost went out of her mind trying to cure it and it just kept spreading. She couldn't keep Janice from scratching!"

A couple of weeks went by and Janice appeared at church one Sunday. She waited until we were alone to talk to Mama and me. She stuck out one leg. "Look, Cousin Jewell," she exclaimed, "You were right! Worked just like you said. The itching stopped right away, but it took the sores longer to heal. The poison ivy left scars cause they were awful deep. I'm so glad you told me what to do! I'll not wait for it to get bad next time."

"I'm glad," Mama replied. "Did you ever tell your mother?"

"Nope! I let her think the last medicine from the doctor worked wonders!"

MY BABY DOLL

The Christmas I was six years old a miracle happened at our house. Santa Claus brought me what I yearned for and had talked about for a long time. Ever since I realized that Christmas was approaching I'd begged for a real doll. That year we children bounced out of bed, as we did each year to see what we had in our stockings. Getting anything else was a most unusual event.

Lying underneath our Christmas tree were two lovely porcelain dolls, with painted cheeks and lips, and eyes that opened and closed. One was for me and the other for my younger sister. I'd never owned a doll before. With squeals of delight I ran to show my mother. "Mama, Mama, look what Santa Claus brought me. A dolly, my very own dolly! Santa Claus brought what I really, really wanted!"

My doll wore a dress, slip, panties and even socks and shoes. To me she was the most wonderful gift in the whole world. "Mama, I think I'll name her Betsy," I said. I played with her every minute, dressing and undressing her, pretending to feed her and hugging her to me as I rocked her to sleep. She was mine, truly mine, and I did not want anyone else to touch her.

Shortly after Christmas, our neighbor, Mrs. Bane, came by to visit and brought her little girl, Lois. "Show Lois your doll, Rita," Mama said, and I held the doll out for her to see and Lois eagerly reached to grab her.

"No!" I pulled back, refusing to share my precious possession.

"Rita," Mama said. "You are a big girl now and must learn to share. Let Lois play with your doll!" Very reluctantly I relinquished my doll.

Lois was only 3 years old. When she tried to undress Betsy she dropped my doll on the wooden floor and broke her head and face. "I told you to be careful," Mrs. Bane said.

I was heart-broken and started crying, "Mama, Mama, I knew Lois was too young to play with Betsy! She is ruined, ruined." Mama tried to comfort me, but I cried myself to sleep that night.

Betsy was the only doll I ever got. She could not be mended and my folks did not have the money to buy me another one.

One Christmas Eve, almost 40 years later, my grown daughter, Sheri, came home from work and handed me a wrapped package. "My friend wants you to have this gift," she said. When I removed the wrappings I found a small doll dressed in a hand-crocheted outfit.

My daughter and I were astonished when I burst into tears and started sobbing. The gift triggered the painful memories of a little girl mourning the loss of her broken doll. The emotional pain deeply buried in my subconscious brought feelings to the surface that shocked and surprised me.

After 40 years I realized that my Christmas doll allowed me to role play motherhood for only a short season of my life. When my daughter presented me with the new doll so many years later, I was shocked to find I was reliving my original hurt about the broken doll. Then God opened my eyes to focus on the immensely greater gift standing before me. I realized that God was allowing me to relinquish my sadness over a long ago broken toy; exchanging it for the ongoing joy I have in the gift of my precious daughter, who from the day she was born, continues to bless me with her life and love.

THE RESCUE

"Mama, can we get a puppy?" I had asked my parents that question many times. My playmates owned a dog, some more than one.

"We'll see." Mama did not say "yes," but her reply gave me hope. When I was young my family never had a pet. Farm children are very fond of animals. The children in our family continued to beg Mama and Daddy to let us get a dog.

One day while playing at the neighbor's house they told us their collie dog had puppies during the night.

"Wouldn't you like one?" They asked. "We're going to give them all away."

They were adorable and I ran home to plead, "Please, please, Mama, can we have a puppy?"

Mama said, "A collie dog would be nice. Let's see what your father thinks."

Daddy said it would be all right, but then added, "You kids will have to take care of your pet."

We promised, and then waited impatiently for the puppy to get old enough to drink milk from a saucer so we could bring him home. Finally that day arrived. We kids took turns holding him in our arms as we walked home carrying the fluffy, adorable little dog we named "Carlo."

We were delighted with our new possession and played with

him constantly. Over and over we threw sticks for him to chase and bring back to us.

One day our family went to chop cotton leaving our puppy in the shade underneath the front porch. When we returned for the noonday meal, we heard pitiful cries mixed with small whining noises. We started running. We knew something was terribly wrong with our little dog. At first we couldn't locate where the noise was coming from. "Mama, where can he be?" we asked.

Everyone looked for him: Underneath the porch, back of the house, in the back yard. We could not find him.

The sound seemed to come from far away. As we followed the whimpering noise we came to our well. We couldn't believe that the sounds seemed to be coming from down deep inside.

"Daddy, Daddy, our doggie is in the well! How could he have gotten there? How are we going to get him out?" We were frantic. We wondered how long Carlo had been in the well and if he could keep swimming until he was rescued.

Some wells in our area were dug by hand and were large at the top. A bucket was let up and down to draw water. However, our well was dug by professional well-drilling equipment and was very small. After drillers reached water they inserted a casing that extended from the water far below to the top of the well. The opening, just above ground level, was about the size of a small pie pan. The space was too small to attempt a rescue. The bucket that drew the water could not be used to rescue the dog. If we let the bucket down, the puppy would be pushed further underneath the water.

Even the smallest person was too large to be lowered into the well. The puppy's cries were getting weaker. We were terrified he might not survive.

"Daddy," I said, "How much longer can Carlo swim without drowning?"

"Honey, I don't know," Daddy answered.

We knew our puppy must be exhausted from trying to keep his head above water. Mama and Daddy were as worried as we were. Something had to be done very quickly.

Daddy thought of a possible solution. "If we had a long fishing line with some huge fishhooks attached, maybe, just maybe, I can hook the dog and pull him out."

Daddy said, "Rita, run to Uncle Claud's house and ask him for a fishing line and his very biggest fishhooks."

Uncle Claud's house was just down the road from where we lived. We did not have a telephone to ask for help, nor a car to drive, so I ran as fast as I possibly could. I was crying as I ran down the dirt road. I didn't stop to knock as we were told to do, but ran right into the house and blurted out my story, telling my uncle to "Hurry, hurry, hurry!"

Uncle Claud rushed to the barn for fishhooks and a fishing line. His legs were longer than mine, so he reached our house ahead of me.

When I got back, the cries had gotten weaker. My father tied two fishhooks to the line and dropped it down into the well. Daddy was hoping the hooks would snag our dog. Once, twice, Daddy jerked the line up and down and nothing caught, but the third time there was weight on the end of the line.

"I've got him!" Daddy said. He carefully started pulling the line up through the small opening. But the hooks had not caught deep enough to hold, and Carlo slipped off into the water again.

Daddy repeated the process. The hooks caught again. We hardly dared to breathe and the cries got louder as the puppy was pulled closer and closer to the top. Then he popped out of the well, fluffy fur soaked flat. One fishhook caught under a front leg and the other on his back.

"He's saved, he's saved!" I squealed with joy as I took the little dog and wrapped him in an old piece of cloth. Carlo was trembling and shaking and making glad little barking noises. He dried in the warm sun while licking the small places where the fishhooks had been removed. The injuries healed nicely.

We never knew how the puppy got into the well. Mama said he probably climbed on top of the cover and somehow knocked the lid aside. We placed a heavier lid on the top and put rocks to hold it secure.

To clean the well, Daddy hauled bucket after bucket of water from the well until the container came up empty. Fresh clean water soon refilled the well.

We enjoyed playing with our dog, Carlo, for many years.

The Unspeakable Act

A s we made our way to the cotton patch, the hot sun appeared on the horizon sending streaks of light across a blue sky. Nothing unusual had happened that week, no foreshadowing of the tragedy that would touch us all.

We worked steadily as we chopped the cotton, thinning out the young plants as we removed the grass and weeds. Our entire family went to the fields to help with this task, working from early morning until late afternoon. We children were too small to chop cotton precisely, for it took good coordination to remove the weeds without uprooting the tender young plants. We went from the end of one long row after another, each child positioned beside one parent to supervise. After an hour of work, we stopped in the shade of the large oak trees for a quick drink of cold water from a glass jug wrapped in burlap. The water alleviated our thirst and the cool shade allowed us to be out of the hot sun for a few brief moments.

"Who can that be coming in this direction?" Mama shaded her eyes against the blinding sun. The lone figure came nearer and we recognized our neighbor whom we called "Mr. Marvin." "Thought he'd be busy planting his corn, what's he doing coming in this direction?"

"Must be something wrong," Daddy replied.

We all stopped hoeing, glad for any interruption in the routine. Mr. Marvin's walk showed a strange urgency as he came toward us and we sensed that this was not a neighbor stopping for a friendly chat. Daddy went a few steps to meet him and I heard an exclamation escape from my father's lips. Whatever the news, it was not good.

The two men came over to where we stood. To my mother's questioning look, my father shook his head, "It's bad, Jewell," he said, and then as if he could not avoid saying the words he blurted, "Marybelle Evans killed her kids!"

"Killed her kids? No! No!" The words came from my mother in a low moan.

Hershel and I stood silent. I thought about what my father had said, but I could not fully grasp the meaning. Children were valued above everything. Mama had told us often, "You are more precious to me than anything in the world." I never once doubted her word.

Jane and Robbie dead? There must be some mistake. A mother would never do that. Something else must have happened to the children. Maybe a misunderstanding, maybe the children were missing and an error had been made in the telling, a horrible story someone told by mistake.

"Oh, God, are you sure?" Mama voiced my thoughts.

"It's true, would to God it was not. The sheriff came and took Marybelle away. The undertaker removed the little bodies."

"Then there's no doubt," my father's voice sounded strange. There seemed nothing left to say. Our family stood and looked at the cotton rows. We made a half-hearted attempt to resume our work, but the hoes felt heavy in our hands and we were without motivation or energy.

"Why don't we all go home," my father dismissed us from even trying to continue. We picked up our hoes and slowly, without talking, made our way to our house.

Everyone knew Marybelle and the family. We did not know of any trouble. The children were beautiful, four and five years old, a boy and a girl. We overheard Mr. Marvin share the gruesome details. We were never shielded from the facts of death and dying. The mother had attempted to take her own life, but found she could not do it. Later we heard that she told her lawyer the children pled for their lives.

The awful news felt like heavy lead in the pit of my stomach. My parents looked sick. The community was terribly shaken and neighbors spoke in hushed whispers, trying to understand what horrible thing had transpired in a mother's mind to cause such an insane act. One by one my parents talked to our neighbors. Everyone was asking the same question, "Why?" I overheard snatches of the conversation among the adults, always spoken in low worried tones.

"Marybelle and Jess had a terrible quarrel that morning. She told him that he would be sorry."

"You mean she would kill the kids to make Jess sorry?"

"I know it's hard to believe. She has to be crazy; no sane person would do a thing like that."

I'd heard of people going crazy, but I had never before heard of a mother who had destroyed her own children. How could this happen to someone in our own small community? Was it possible that one of my parents would do a thing like that? The thought was unbearable. As I glanced at my parents I felt reassured. They loved me.

I closed my eyes and tried to imagine being dead. Even though I knew about Heaven, where I would go when I died, I could not imagine that Jane and Robbie were there now, playing and happy. All I could see was blackness and nothingness where there had once been joy and love.

We attended all funerals and were taken to the services by our parents. Everyone went; babies in their mother's arms, young kids like me, young couples dating, married people such as my parents, and elderly grandparents.

The dreadful day for this funeral was no exception. We went to the graveyard in the horse-drawn wagon and we children sat in the floor on an old quilt. My folks stopped by to pick up the neighbors to ride with us. The adults sat in the wagon seats up front.

I dressed in my Sunday clothing, a bright print dress that my aunt had sewn for me and I wore shiny black patent leather shoes. My family wore their very best clothing. It was not considered "fittin' and proper" to dress in any other way.

As we stood together waiting for the family and hearse to arrive, the graveyard bell that stood on a wooden platform near the center of the graveyard, tolled for the children—four brief peals for Jane, and then after a short interval, 5 peals for Robbie, then silence. In the past I had heard the bell rung for older people and my brother and I would count off the number of rings, telling us how old the person had been.

The sheriff said the mother would not be allowed to attend the funeral. She had been taken to see the children when they were ready for burial. We were told she patted their cheeks and said, "They look very sweet and beautiful." She showed no remorse.

The black hearse arrived followed by the black car that carried the family members. I heard people crying aloud as the two small white caskets were carried to an area near the open gravesite. The father's head hung in sorrow, his face showing the pain of his loss. Relatives supported him on either side.

Our minister, Brother West, led the short service. He asked that we bow our heads as he prayed for the Lord to comfort the family, that He forgive us our sins, that He give us love for one another, and that we be able to say "Thy will be done." As he prayed, tears and perspiration mingled running down his face, which he continually wiped with a large white handkerchief.

He read the names of the children, their ages, and the family survivors, and ended the service by quoting the Scripture, "And they shall hunger no more, neither thirst any more … for the Lord will be their shepherd … and God will wipe away every tear from their eyes."

We all stood in the little country cemetery and cried together. I cried for the dead children because I knew there would be no more hugs and kisses and goodnight prayers for Jane and Robbie. I cried for the daddy and mommy who would never again hear the sweet voices or see the perfectly formed bodies. I cried for the bright children's eyes with the long, dark lashes now closed forever.

As the minister finished his remarks the undertaker stepped forward and opened the caskets for viewing. A line was formed and the people slowly passed by. Daddy lifted me up so I could see my little friends, who looked as if they had fallen asleep while dressed for church. The marks of their cruel death were no longer evident, except for a small piece of adhesive tape that barely showed underneath Robbie's chin.

The service was over, but we did not leave until the small caskets were gently lowered into a double grave. The men shoveled the hard clay dirt into the deep hole, rounding the top into two short mounds that were then covered by flowers.

My world would never be quite the same again. Nothing further could be done, but we were reluctant to leave. The following day we took up our tasks where they had been interrupted. For some time, mothers and fathers were noticeably more soft-spoken and considerate of one another and their children.

* Actual names were changed in this account

A Season To Remember

Seven years old in 1934, I looked forward to choosing our Christmas tree. My brother, sister, and I searched for a perfect cedar as we walked through the fields and forest on the land my father farmed. As sharecroppers in our rural area of Arkansas we could choose any tree we liked. Our neighbors in the small communities near Morrilton, where Daddy did the grocery shopping, did not buy trees. No one bought trees. I cannot remember a single Christmas tree lot.

"Look," Hershel pointed to a small evergreen. "There's one that might do."

"Looks too small to me," Opal said.

"Can't be too big. Wouldn't fit in our house," I replied. "Let's keep that one in mind while we continue looking. We may find a better one." We finally settled on a small tree that would fit on top of the desk section of the cherished bookcase made by Great Grandfather William Henry Miller.

A couple of days before the holiday my siblings and I took the axe and followed the toe path through the woods to cut the tree chosen earlier. After Hershel chopped the tree down, he carried our prize home, while Opal and I tagged along behind.

"Mama," I called. "Come see our perfect tree."

We fashioned trimmings of paper chains by coloring between the lines of a writing tablet, cutting them into strips, and fastening the links with paste made from flour. Candy and cigarette packages provided foil for icicles. We added popcorn and chinaberry seeds strung with a needle and thread.

"Wouldn't it be nice if we had snow?" I asked that question every year. But snow rarely fell in our part of the south. We always hoped for a white Christmas, but instead we were often greeted by biting cold with ground frozen solid.

Early in the afternoon of Christmas Eve, dark clouds hovered while the temperature dropped. Hershel raced into the house exclaiming, "Come and look, it's beginning to snow!" We hurried outside to see white flakes drifting silently down from the sky. "Wonderful!" I exclaimed. "Looks like we may have a white Christmas!" We kids ran around and around with our arms outstretched in the magical world of white as we watched the tiny flakes melt when they touched the ground. The snow fell faster as darkness descended.

Christmas dawn we awakened to the bang, bang of firecrackers—a common custom for greeting the holiday. I hopped out of bed to see what Santa Claus brought and stopped short when I saw our tree. A light dusting of snow covered the tree branches. I reached out to touch the delicate flakes, felt them melt against my fingers.

I ran to tell my family, "There's real snow on our Christmas tree."

Mama said, "Wind must've blown the snow between the boards into the house. The cracks are bigger than we thought."

I peered out the window. Our unpainted buildings and dirt road were changed to an enchanting land of white perfection.

I then checked my stocking to see what Santa brought and found an apple, an orange, some nuts and hard candy, things we rarely had except at Christmas.

We hardly had time to eat breakfast before voices sounded

at our door. We heard the same greeting year-after-year used by grown-ups and kids alike. "Christmas gift," my cousins, Helen and Ellen, shouted. I replied with the customary response, "Give it here." In reality no gift was given or expected.

I looked past the twins and heard squeals of laughter that echoed in the stillness as snowballs splattered those who failed to dodge. Neighbors slipped and slid playing with their children. Mama and Daddy, whom I considered far too old for snow fights, joined the action. We were giddy with laughter as we engaged in the fun.

"I'll make you some snow cream before the snow melts," Mama said. We used large spoons to scoop the fragile delicacy from the top of a wooden fence and into a container. Mama added sugar and a dollop of vanilla flavoring with a bit of real cream. We savored the cool, smooth treat as it melted in our mouths. "Tastes like real ice cream," I said, as my siblings agreed.

As the day came to an end, Mama tucked her children under the patchwork quilts upon the feather bed. She heated flat irons in the fireplace and wrapped them in flannel to warm our feet.

Before I drifted off to sleep, I thought about the joyful events: snowflakes gently falling and leaving unexpected decoration on our tree, awakening to perfect scenery, and best of all, families participating in gleeful play. Each scene left a precious memory, like a prized snapshot in an old family album.

THE STYLISH HAIRCUT

"Rita, your hair needs cutting again." Mama reached out to pat my shining hair.

"Please, Mama, let it grow long, like yours!" I pled with her as I had done many times in the past, even though I knew from experience that she would probably again say, "No."

"Honey, it'd be too much trouble, too hard to wash and comb the tangles out. Besides that, it's too hot and sweaty to have long hair in the summertime."

"But Mama, I wouldn't care how hot it was. You could curl my hair like Emma Jean's. Her mother puts her hair up in rags almost every night and the long curls are so pretty."

Mama sighed softly, "Not now, Rita, but someday, I promise, we'll let your hair grow long for curls." Then she went to get the hair-cutting scissors. Mama cut straight across the front to form the bangs and then circled around the back and sides. I hated my haircut and avoided looking at myself in the mirror.

Mama wore her beautiful hair like a lovely crown. Her hair was her best feature, dark and heavy with enough curl to wave softly. When she worked in the hot kitchen, tiny curls sprang from the sides to frame her face. At the end of the day I watched as she removed the large combs and pins and let her hair drop down her back while she brushed the thick, soft mass. Often in the early morning lamplight I saw Daddy watching her as she put her hair up, winding it around her head.

For as long as I could remember, I had wished for long, curly hair like Mama's. Instead, my hair was absolutely straight and as soon as it grew the least bit long, Mama would cut it again. I just kept hoping that the "someday" she had promised me would arrive soon.

Mama did not tell Daddy the day she decided to have her hair cut. She told me she had something special planned and that I could go with her. I thought it strange that she didn't tell Daddy where we were going, for she usually told him everything. I was shocked when I found that we were entering the barbershop. I watched with mounting anxiety as Mama sat in the big barber chair. The barber asked her what he could do for her and I heard Mama say, "I've come for a haircut."

I wanted to scream "No, no!," but the shock of the action kept me from a word of protest. The barber looked a bit surprised. "You're sure you want me to cut your long hair?"

Mama nodded her head. "Oh, yes," she said. "I want it cut. Real short. A stylish bob the same as my friend, Rachel. You cut her hair and I like it a lot."

I gasped as the barber took down the big scissors and quickly cut off the long strands, letting them fall on the floor in a big heap. He then took smaller scissors and shingled the hair up the back, leaving it longer on either side over the ears, and finished by using the clippers at the back of the neck. He then handed my mother a mirror. "I like it," she said.

The appalling deed happened quickly. I slowly gathered the thick hair from the floor and stood holding it in my hands until the barber handed me a brown paper sack. I lovingly touched the soft hair as I gently dropped it inside the sack while a lump in my throat threatened to choke me. Mama paid the barber and we left the shop.

"What'll Daddy say?" I asked as we walked home. I knew in my heart that Daddy was not going to like the short hair. "Don't ever bob your hair," I'd heard him say more than once. I felt terrible because Mama had not told Daddy her plan.

"He'll get used to it," Mama replied.

After we arrived home we stayed very busy the rest of the afternoon, straightening the house and preparing food for dinner. But in between all the work I noticed that Mama's hands were pulling the short hair at the sides of her face, especially as she watched the time for Daddy to come home from plowing in the field.

As the hour grew nearer, her hands fluttered nervously about her face and she glanced uneasily into the small mirror that hung in the kitchen. "I'm home!" Daddy called, as he flung the door open. For a moment he seemed unable to move, his eyes wide with disbelief. "Jewell, what did you do to your hair?" he screamed at my mother. I wondered why he was asking such a dumb question for he could clearly see what she had done.

"Now, Arthur," Mama said quietly, "Everyone is having their hair bobbed these days."

"Everyone? Everyone? Then everyone is crazy! What do you want to be? A man? Well, that's exactly what you look like! Next thing you know, you'll be wanting to wear pants!" And then he did something I had never before seen my father do. He cried, tears slowly cruising down his cheeks. He then turned and ran out of the house.

Now, I knew why my mother had not told him that she was planning to cut her hair. She would never have had the nerve to withstand my father's outrage.

Mama and we three kids were in the house without Daddy that night. We ate in silence the good dinner Mama had prepared and I might as well have eaten straw for all the enjoyment it gave me.

I noticed that Mama hardly ate anything. Later I helped Mama as we washed the supper dishes. While she scrubbed the plates, silverware, and pans she taught me a popular song, "Why Do You Bob Your Hair, Girls?"

Mama laughed as she sang the song, poking fun at the words. As we worked Mama kept watching the door. Her smile sought to assure me she was happy with her decision.

I thought that God probably did not care whether my mother's hair was long or short, but I couldn't erase from my mind the picture of my father crying. "Please God," I prayed that night kneeling beside my bed, "Let Mama's hair grow long again, and make my daddy come back home."

The next morning when I awoke, I heard my father and mother talking in low voices. Their voices were restrained and somehow much different from normal. I lay still thinking about the quarrel and feeling glad that Daddy was back home. When I could no longer hear them talking, I knew Daddy had gone to the barn to milk the cows. I crawled out of bed when I smelled the bacon frying in the iron skillet and knew the biscuits were baking in the oven. Mama's eyes were red, but she nodded her head "Yes" to my question, "Mama, are you all right?"

My father came from the barn carrying the pails full of warm, foaming milk. He sat them down on the shelf and then removed his old straw hat. I stared. Daddy's head was as smooth-shaven as his face. Not a single hair was left.

"Do you like my new haircut, little girl?" he asked as he ran his hand over his bald head. I shook my head, "Oh, Daddy, it looks terrible! What does Mama think?"

"Why don't you ask her," my father replied.

"Mama, do you like Daddy's bald head?" My world seemed upside down.

"I think that I better not say," Mama replied while gazing out the window.

"Well," Daddy said, "Like your mother told me about her haircut, someday my hair will grow back!"

My Grandmother Miller always said "Two wrongs don't make a right." If my parents had forgiven one another, I would have felt much better.

I don't know whether Daddy ever accepted Mama having her hair bobbed, for he went around giving Mama the silent treatment for what seemed like weeks-on-end. Not only did Daddy continue to shave his head, he also let his beard grow out. Eventually Mama allowed her hair to grow long again and she wore it that way for many years.

I doubt that God decided to mete out punishment for Daddy's actions, but a quirk of nature added irony to life's story when my father became quite bald at an early age for the remainder of his life.

You'll Be Sorry

The year was punctuated by periods of anxiety about my father's health. Early in winter he slipped in the muddy barnyard. In trying to catch his balance, he grabbed for a nearby post and caught his hand on a rusty meat hook. The injury left a deep, wide gash that he insisted upon doctoring with Epsom salts dissolved in hot water. I knew my parents were concerned about infection. I overheard them talk about watching for red stripes running up his arm. However, the wound healed nicely.

Several months later when cutting wood, Daddy misjudged the direction a tree would fall. A big limb knocked him to the ground. Bruised and badly shaken by the accident, he limped around for months, insisting that nothing was broken.

Later he developed a hacking cough. Over and over Mama urged him to see a doctor. "It's nothing," he told her. "Just a little cold." Instead of getting better, the cough persisted, but Daddy continued working as usual.

Our family gathered in the yard to watch Daddy build a birdhouse in the big tree near the house. Hershel and I had pestered him about building a birdhouse for several weeks. Spring arrived and birds flew around looking for a place to build nests. Daddy wanted to encourage the birds. He talked to us about what wonderful insect eaters the wrens and martins were, especially when baby birds hatched. Although Daddy was a busy man, he yielded to our urging and took time off from the spring plowing to build the birdhouse.

He had climbed the high ladder when two women dressed in bright clothing came walking down the dirt road. All of us watched the two strangers. As they approached I saw they had dark skin and wore bright long skirts and gold earrings.

Mama whispered to us, "Those women are gypsies."

We children had never seen gypsies before and were full of questions: "Who are gypsies? What are they doing here? What do they want?"

"They're people who travel around from place to place and tell fortunes," Mama answered.

"Tell fortunes? What's that?"

"They try to tell what's going to happen to a person."

"Can they really do that, Mama?

"Shhh-they'll hear you. Let's see what they want."

The gypsies turned into our yard and asked if they could tell our fortunes.

Mama said, "No, we do not want our fortunes told."

We were startled when they started describing Daddy's personality. "You've got a quick temper," they said, "and you always insist on having your own way."

She was right in everything. Daddy's face turned bright red. We children were intrigued and started begging, "Please, Daddy, let the gypsies tell your fortune!"

"No!" Daddy's eyes flashed. "Don't have money for such a thing!"

The older gypsy responded. "Fella like you should have your fortune told! You work too hard and too fast!" Every word was true. We wondered how she knew.

"Person has to work hard to take care of his family!"

"But you've been too tired. And you've been coughing a lot."

"It's just a little cough. Don't mean nothin'." Daddy answered firmly.

"Not so, not so! Anyone in your family have tuberculosis?"

"My health is fine!" Daddy answered a bit too quickly and fear must have gripped his heart. His sister, Clara, was dying of tuberculosis.

"I see darkness in your future. You give me a little money, I can cure that for you."

"Don't have money to spend on such a thing. Got no money for fortune tellers!" I could tell that Daddy was angry. But we children started pleading with him anyway, "Please Daddy, let them help you!" I noticed the straight hard line of his mouth and knew he would never relent.

"I'll make you well, just take a few dollars." The gypsy persisted.

"I've got no money!" my father retorted.

"Oh, yes, you have. I see money buried close by!" As the words were said my father glanced quickly at my mother. No one was supposed to know that they had managed to save a little money.

I could tell my parents' wished to get rid of the gypsies and their terrible forecast of evil. My father's voice was sharp as he said, "Don't have anything else to say on the matter. Good day to you!" He turned his back and starting hammering loudly up in the tree.

The older gypsy shook her head, "Too bad. I could cure you for just a little money." Then as they were turning to go, the younger one looked at us and said, "You'll be sorry!"

My father waited impatiently until he was sure the gypsies were gone before he came down from the tree and went straight to the milk shed to dig up the fruit jar with his entire savings.

"Do you think they'll be back?" I asked my mother.

"I don't think so. They like to go where people pay to have their fortunes told." I felt she was trying to reassure us.

The gypsies appalling prediction may have been in my parents' thoughts as they went about their work. Daddy's cough got worse. Mama must have listened, terrified during the long nights. When she pleaded with him to see a doctor he'd say, "I'm feeling a little puny. I'll soon feel much better," and he kept right on working as hard as ever.

Then my father's sister, Clara, died of tuberculosis and during that sad time for all the family, my Daddy's cough continued. He still had trouble, a year or so after her death. No one ever convinced him to see a doctor. He just kept saying, "Cost too much money. I'll soon be all right!"

Eventually the cough got better and then it went away completely. He told Mama, "I knew I would be all right. Always have!"

Many years later, Mama watched as Daddy picked up heavy sacks of feed for the barnyard animals, no doubt marveling at his strength and agility. At seventy, Daddy remained a strong man, capable of doing a full day's work on the farm. I knew Mama worried many times when Daddy seemed ill, but would never see a doctor. However, his body evidently healed by positive thinking, faith, time, and sheer determination.

Mama may have thought about the long-ago visit by the gypsies, but she never mentioned it to her family. Their prediction that she and Daddy's lives would be marred by ill health and bad fortune never came true. They survived the depression years and managed to prosper and save for their old age, living into their 90's.

SUDDEN SORROW

During a hot, humid day in early fall we are working in our cotton field side by side, black and white. My father is pleased that he's been able to hire the Payne family to help us. They are reliable hard workers, who can be depended upon to be there when they promised. They waited to arrive until after the dew dried. They have now been picking steadily for several hours. My father, mother, brother, and I have worked shortly after the early morning dawn. At that time the air was cooler and the flour-sack jacket that I wear for protection against the sun, felt comfortable in the cool air.

Now that the hired help has arrived, the picking will go much faster. What a magnificent family they are! I watch to see if Lizzie, a girl my own age, is among them. I'm greeted with a welcoming smile. She and I play together when there is a break in the routine, a few minutes during the noon hour and at the end of the day.

My older brother, Hershel, teases both of us, pretending he'll hit us with the clods of dirt or dried cotton bolls being thrown in our direction. I tolerate his teasing. I'm used to it, but I'm furious that he teases Lizzie.

"Don't you tease my friend!" I yell at him, but he pays no attention until Daddy tells him to stop.

From the youngest to old "Uncle Jim" the whole family appears joyful. They work diligently and are given very few instructions and no supervision. They spread out, the older ones picking two rows each, while the young children pick from a single row. Their soft, mellow voices can be heard laughing and talking from time to time. They work swiftly, deftly removing the cotton from each boll, leaving it clean-picked, no "goose-locks" or ragged rows left behind.

The sun beats down relentlessly in a clear, cloudless blue sky and the temperature climbs into the nineties. Since the weather has turned so hot the cotton bolls have opened rapidly, leaving a vast field of white ready for the harvest. Each of us, other than the smaller children, pulls a long canvas sack made with a strap over the shoulder with an opening at the top to deposit the picked cotton. Occasionally one of the little ones can be seen "hitching" a ride on the back of a sack as it is being pulled along.

The work is hard and back-breaking. Each cotton boll is picked separately by hand and we take care to have clean-picked cotton without debris from dried twigs or cotton leaves. The workers pick rapidly and steadily, filling the long sacks to be taken to the scales and weighed. Occasionally a lone voice is raised in song, and then other voices join in harmony. The music is beautiful, haunting, and it often sounds sad to me.

The temperature stifles us, and the humidity makes the day more uncomfortable. The sacks are almost full and weighing time will soon be called. Far across the way a solitary figure comes running, and everyone stops and waits, breathless, anxious, but not moving. The messenger approaches "Uncle Jim" and whispers his message. The elderly black man shakes his head and whispers a message to the person closest to him. With soft wailing of voices, followed by low moaning groans, word flashes from mouth to mouth. With one accord, in unison, and without any additional words being spoken, each of the workers; men, women, and children remove their picking sack and leave it where they are standing. They depart immediately, cutting straight across the fields and fence rows and fast disappearing into the woods, seeking the shortest path home.

My father's face expresses sadness as he goes about picking up the sacks that are left. He carries them to the scales to be weighed. As he reads the weight for each sack, he writes a careful notation in the record-keeping notebook.

I am greatly puzzled by the sudden departure of our workers, and I ask my father what happened. He gently explains to me that the elderly grandmother, "Uncle Jim's wife" has suddenly passed away. I think of the sound of their grief and the abrupt leave-taking, and find that I, too, am touched by their sorrow.

As a sign of respect, Daddy stops work in the fields to attend the service. Several white folks who knew "Aunt Bessie" for many years were also at her funeral, sitting in a back row reserved for them.

The hired crew will be away for several days, returning after the funeral to fulfill their promise.

POSTPONEMENT OF A DREAM

My great uncle Claud Griswood, his wife Pet, and six daughters—Sybil, Myrtis, Ordell, Mary Dale, and the twins, Helen and Ellen—lived less than one-half mile down the dirt road from us. Rarely a day went by without me playing with the twins, my age.

Their makeshift house provided temporary shelter until a new house could be built. The large wooden kitchen extended to a screened-in sleeping porch, fine for the summer, cold in the winter. On the other side, an enormous canvas tent, permanently installed over a bare wooden floor, was held in place by a center beam and corner posts. The tent served as a multi-purpose room for living and sleeping. One corner partitioned off by heavy canvas provided privacy to dress, or to bathe from a pitcher of water poured into a tin wash pan.

The identical twins had sandy-blonde hair, greenish eyes and fair skin that blistered in the sun. With my olive skin, blue eyes, and dark hair, I provided a great contrast, not only in looks, but in personality.

Helen and Ellen, a fun loving duo, appeared bent on mischief. One day they lured me into scaling the ladder-like wall to the tall loft of their barn. As I climbed near the top rung, my foot slipped and I fell to the ground below, hitting a wagon tongue that knocked me out. They ran to get their big sister who carried me to our house. Remarkably, I was not injured or killed.

The twins were totally without fear of all living creatures. In addition, they climbed the highest trees, hanging upside down by their heels from the limbs. I thought them daring and brave for I was leery of bugs, snakes, animals, and high places.

Helen and Ellen boasted to me one day that their daddy planned to build a beautiful new house. Few people had money to build houses in our area, but I believed them completely.

The neighbors discussed Uncle Claud's desire to build, "as soon as the money is available." At one time the house seemed close to reality when trees were felled in the bottomland and hauled to the sawmill for cutting. We children played on the stacked lumber by the edge of the road, climbing up, over, and around the pieces, and jumping off the top of the high stack.

Soon after the lumber arrived, Ellen told me, "Daddy says we can start building soon." Helen added, "It's going to be a wonderful big house with lots of bedrooms and a real bathroom."

I was happy for them, but I also felt envious. My family still lived in the sharecropper's two-room, unpainted shack. We had no immediate plans for a different house, although my father talked about his dream of buying his own farm.

Uncle Claud inherited his land from my great grandfather and was considered wealthy by our standards. But earning enough money to feed and clothe a large family took careful management.

The Griswood family never complained about their house. An embroidered framed motto "God Bless This Home" hung in the living area, and they seemed confident that He would do just that, provided certain rules were followed that pleased the Lord.

The official enforcers of the strict code were my aunt and uncle, who told us the Lord did not like girls wearing pants, bobbed hair, or lipstick. He did not like daughters who "talked back" to their parents, had idle hands, or hung around boys. The

Lord did not want children to squirm in church or use slang words that sounded like cussing. He wanted people to praise Him in song, but not in dance, to practice cleanliness and order, wasting not one thing, including fried chicken feet.

Year after year my friends talked about the new house, as we played together on the lumber piles. "This is really good-seasoned lumber. It'll build the best house around," the twins often told me.

One day my father announced Uncle Claud planned an addition to his enormous barn, as soon as the crops were "laid by" during the slow period before harvest started.

"But I thought the lumber was to build a house!" I protested.

"Oh, yes, that's true," Daddy said, "There'll be plenty of lumber left, but some things have to come first."

My father reminded our family he wanted to buy a farm with a large barn. He worked long hours when other farmers quit at the end of the day.

The years marched by. "When is Uncle Claud going to start building the house?" I asked the twins, hoping that the answer would be "this very day." But the house remained a dream.

We attended church regularly. The Griswood family contributed a tithe, one-tenth of their income, to the Lord. Uncle Claud's comparatively large offerings made the building of a new church possible, but I felt a new house much more important.

Still, Uncle Claud and Aunt Pet prospered. They bought farm equipment, a new team of horses and increased the cattle in their herd. They raised hogs to slaughter and grew vegetables for fresh produce in summer and canned food for winter.

All of the girls helped with farm work, the older ones worked alongside their father. "Sybil and Ordell can pitch hay like a man!" Daddy said.

When I was eight years old we moved to another farm.

However, we visited the Griswoods often. My aunt and uncle opened their home to friends and strangers. I was often invited to eat Sunday dinner and joined assorted guests and relatives. I wished for fewer people there; we kids spent long hours washing dishes after the large meal.

While visiting one day, Helen and Ellen asked me to go across the road to a small knoll. "This is the spot!" they said. "We're going to build our house here!"

When I was nine years old, a Bible conference in the Ozark Mountains was announced at church. I listened to the plans without hope of attending. I was astonished when Uncle Claud paid my way. He placed the camp fees in my hand plus five dollars for spending money. I'd never before had any money and five dollars represented a fortune to me in 1936 during the Great Depression.

I felt a great affection for my uncle and aunt for their generosity. I loved the camping experience and remember the words to our theme song, "Looking unto Him, Who can save from sin and misery. Looking unto Him, He's the dearest friend for you and me!"

Everyone was surprised when we moved to our own farm when I was eleven. The farm belonged to my mother's parents and one-tenth of the property was my mother's inheritance. By pinching pennies and working days and into the night, my father scraped together enough money over years to later buy the other 9/10ths of the original Chandler farm. Our new home was an imposing structure with dormer windows, built many years before and never modernized. It did not matter, we were glad to call the place our own.

During the following years, my uncle's daughters left home one by one. After attending college, Sybil left for nurses' training in Memphis. Since money was practically non-existent, we were amazed that her family could afford the tuition.

Bits of information filtered back of her struggle to manage on meager sums. One day a letter arrived from Sybil. She added a postscript to her dad. "You said you were enclosing a dollar, but I can't find it. Could you please send one soon?"

At some point, Helen and Ellen took me once more to the site for the new house. Stakes were hammered into place outlining the shape, while string marked off the rooms. They pointed out the bathroom and kitchen, and told me they would have running water and electricity.

Myrtis graduated from high school and she and Ordell left to help in the war effort. Ellen quit school and married before her 17th birthday. For several years after high school, Helen remained home to help with the farm work. Mary Dale married a local boy in the Navy. Mrytis married a serviceman and returned home where she bore a daughter, then two years later, a son.

Uncle Claud and Aunt Pet doted on their first grandchildren. Myrtis had grown accustomed to the conveniences of living in town and voiced her dislike for the tent house.

Over two decades after the lumber had been cut, construction started.

In 1949, the long-delayed dream became a reality. By that time, I had married and lived in California. My mother wrote, "You should visit Aunt Pet and Uncle Claud when you come home. I know they want you to see their new house."

Daddy drove me to visit my uncle and aunt. The house, located in the area I once lived, could be seen from the country road. A dirt driveway led to the porch bordered by flowerbeds of bright zinnias and marigolds. The building stood on the exact spot shown to me as a child. I had envisioned a lofty mansion; instead I found a modest farmhouse.

My aunt and uncle greeted me affectionately. "Rita, we wondered if you might come to see us," Uncle Claud said. "We thought you might have forgotten us."

I shook my head as I fought back the tears, "You are two people I could never forget!" I hugged them tightly and kissed their wrinkled cheeks.

"Let me show you the house," Aunt Pet said, taking me through the four bedrooms, a single bathroom, and a kitchen with modern equipment. Small rugs lay on the living room floor of polished hardwood. The furniture appeared the same as I remembered.

After I viewed the house, Uncle Claud, his gruff voice breaking with emotion, said, "Our greatest pleasure in life has been seeing our children grow to mature adults. This house is a luxury that we never really missed. We thank God for blessing us so abundantly."

The School Bus Driver

T he scrawny little man with a mustache and a sour disposition appeared an unlikely candidate to drive our school bus. I suspect no other person applied for the job. Everyone called him Johnny Walker, grownups and school kids alike, and that was strange, for we were taught to call married people Mister or Miz. We kids thought of him as old, but in reality, he probably was less than thirty when I started to school.

In contrast, his wife Miz Lena was a quiet, gentle woman, very tall and large, who taught first grade and gave piano lessons after school to students who could pay. I was not in that group, for money was too scarce and we barely afforded pencils, writing paper and Crayolas.

The bus arrived each day on schedule, dependable as daybreak. The school district provided no relief bus driver and I never knew Johnny Walker to take time off because of sickness. He appeared regularly year after year without worker benefits—vacation, sick time, health or retirement. He drove for several years before I started school and continued long past the normal age to retire.

The school bus route ran along the paved highway. To reach it, my brother and I walked a mile and a half on dirt road—muddy and slippery in the winter and hot and dusty in the summer. In wet weather my clothes were soaked and my shoes leaked. In winter my hands and legs turned blue from the cold and I could hardly control the chattering of my teeth and the shaking of my body. I stomped my feet to try to warm them against the freezing air and tried to walk faster or run from time to time. If my brother and I reached the bus stop early, we found no protection against the weather. In summer the heat waves enveloped me as I trudged home on the dusty road. But I loved the springtime, when the dogwood and redbud started to bloom, and the sky turned blue with white clouds drifting overhead.

Even in the coldest weather, I went off to school in cotton dresses made by my aunt. I wore an old coat given to me by a relative who lived in town. My shoes were inexpensive oxfords worn with anklets which left my legs bare. In contrast with the tow-headed kids with whom I played, my shiny, dark hair hung straight, cut with bangs across my forehead.

I carried my lunch of home-made biscuits with a slice of ham or fresh side pork, wrapped in newspaper. I had no fruit, potato chips or goodies that I saw some of the other kids eating. During rain or snow, I held my lunch, books, and writing paper under my coat.

The bus was ancient, slow and uncomfortable, fitted with hard wooden benches and without any heat. Whenever my brother and I heard the bus laboring up the hill, we ran the last few yards. Johnny Walker waited for us, but he muttered his displeasure. When we were within sight he blew the horn, urging us to run faster.

"Hurry and sit down," he yelled as we got on the bus.

"Wonder why Johnny Walker's always so mad? Guess maybe Miz Lena wouldn't sleep with him last night!" Jim, the smart aleck kid in the sixth grade, started whispering. Other kids joined in with snorts and giggles.

"Quiet down, back there!" Johnny Walker thundered, naming the offenders one by one. We kids immediately hushed talking and everyone sat still as statues. We did not dare look at one another, for fear someone might snicker again.

Our bus driver knew each child by name and his family history. Rumors spread that he provided financial help for families who suffered a run of bad luck. But we found it hard to believe, and most of the children feared him. He often threatened us with dire acts of violence if we misbehaved. "I'll cut off your nose and ears if you do that again!" and to emphasize his point he would grab the hatchet he always carried in the front of the bus. Not many children disobeyed him for long. Especially not me, for I never thought of defying anyone in authority.

While riding on the school bus we were not allowed to talk, sing, change seats, laugh or tease. One day my cousin Audrey dared break the rules and insisted on talking to her best friend.

"Quit that talking, Audrey Spier!" Johnny Walker roared. But Audrey was high-spirited and fun-loving and soon disobeyed the order.

"I'm warning you, Audrey, you quit talking or I'll put you off this bus!" Johnny watched her, as he glared into the huge mirror mounted above the driver's seat.

Audrey stayed silent for a few minutes, but soon remembered what she wanted to say and started to whisper again. Johnny braked suddenly as he pulled the bus over and stopped on the side of the road.

"Okay, Audrey Spier. I told you to stop talking. Now you are going to walk the rest of the way home! Get off!"

Horrified that Johnny planned to carry out his threat, I watched as Audrey made her way to the front and slowly got off the bus. I could hardly believe that our bus driver would make her walk the rest of the way home. Not a single child pled for him to reconsider as the bus pulled away. Audrey's regular bus stop was only a mile or so further, and no one considered it dangerous to walk alone in our community.

When my cousin did not arrive home at the usual hour, Aunt Altie checked with other youngsters and found out Audrey was walking home. Her parents did not complain about the incident. As far as I know, no one ever challenged the authority or actions of our bus driver.

To drive an old bus on slick roads was hazardous. When it started to snow, the ice began forming on the windshield. Johnny Walker stopped the bus and took out two small candles, which he lighted and placed in holders on the dashboard. The flickering warmth created two small spots that allowed him to peer out to see the road. In all those years the bus was never involved in an accident.

The one bright spot for having Johnny Walker as our bus driver happened every Christmas. As we entered the bus on the last day of school before the holiday, we smelled oranges and apples and knew that he planned his yearly treat. As the children left the bus on the return trip home, each child was handed a red mesh bag shaped like a stocking, containing an apple, an orange, some candy and nuts. "Merry Christmas!" Johnny's joyful greeting rang over and over. He appeared to watch for each child's face to light up as hands reached to receive the treasure.

Forty years after my high school graduation, my son David represented my family by attending a homecoming held in the Arkansas community where I grew up. He took his video camera to film the many people that I might remember. Upon his return home, David was eager to show me the pictures he made.

As he ran the film he suddenly exclaimed, "Look, Mom, Grandpa said that man drove your school bus when you were young!" There on the screen was a little shriveled-up man, now missing an arm, but unmistakably Johnny Walker. He stood near a group of little children and watched with obvious enjoyment as they played together.

My Baby Brother

~~~~~~~◆~◆~◆~~~~~~~

S hortly after my ninth birthday, I noticed a difference in
Mama. She seemed overly tired and sleepy. Herschel and I
helped with the work more than usual: washing dishes, clearing
the table, drawing water from the well, and bringing in wood
for the fireplace and cook stove. I did not realize my mother
desperately needed my support, for she did not confide the reason
for her fatigue.

Instead of preparing me for the new baby she expected, she
left me to puzzle over what was happening. I withdrew and created
little problems to draw attention: a splinter in my finger needed
removing, my stomach hurt, my shoes were too short.

Someone eventually told me, "Your mother is expecting a
baby" or I figured it out for myself. Because Mama weighed more
than most women, her pregnancy was hidden for several months.

I did not understand my anger, although adding to our family
increased financial worries and our income continued to be
almost non-existent. We occupied the tenant house on Grandpa
Chandler's farm, an unpainted shack with two rooms and a
"lean-to" enclosed for a third room.

I dared not ask either parent about the baby. When I found
out Mama was expecting, no one would talk about it. We never
talked about such things to one another. Instead, I became
increasingly moody and difficult. I wanted my parents to know of
my disapproval. A visiting nurse came by the house occasionally

and we children were sent outside to play. I wanted to go back inside to see what was happening, and picked at a finger until it bled for an excuse to interrupt the exam.

Looking back, I wonder if jealously contributed to feelings of hostility about my sister, Opal. I do not remember her birth, for I was not quite two years old when she was born. Mama repeatedly told me, "Take good care of your baby sister." Daddy carried her when we walked long distances. I may have felt I was pushed out of the nest too soon in having to share my parents.

Years later, Mama told me that Daddy focused what little leisure time he had on me. She rebuked him: "You give Rita too much attention." According to Mama, he never again took me with him. I was saddened to think that the special relationship with my Daddy disappeared after Mama's ill-fated advice. I must have realized at that time that Daddy was not as mindful of me.

Finally after months of waiting, Daddy shook me awake. "Wake up, wake up. I'm taking you kids to Aunt Tennie's for the rest of the night." She and Uncle Alec lived in the big house on the Chandler farm. Early the next morning we ate breakfast and caught the school bus. I wanted to know what happened at our house. Had the baby been born? Was my mother all right? Did I have a brother or a sister? Why weren't we told before my aunt sent us to school?

I waited impatiently throughout the long day, hardly thinking of anything except events occurring at home. The bell finally rang, dismissing school. The bus crept along on the return trip. As soon as I got off at our regular bus stop, I ran as fast as possible on the dirt road to our house.

I burst into the room and saw Mama lying in the bed holding a tiny baby with lots of black hair, dark eyes, and a red face. I walked over for a closer look and instantly fell in love with the little person; perfect, helpless, and completely dependent on our care.

I have no idea how Mama and Daddy chose the name Lewis Earl, but then I never knew how they selected any of our names. A rather strange list it seemed to me. Everyone called me "Rita" and I never heard anything different until I started to school and found my birth certificate showed "Loretta." We did not call our new baby by his real name for long. He became "Buddy" to almost everyone.

I was annoyed when one of the relatives teased, "I think you named your new baby after the prize fighter Joe Lewis!" At that time, white people in the South would not name their children for anyone who was black, not even a famous person. Our baby's middle name was for Daddy's youngest brother, although he and my father were not close.

From the first day Buddy was born, his cry meant instant attention from the entire family. We vied for who would hold and take care of him. Mama trusted me to rock him to sleep. I did not bathe him, but I changed diapers. The wet ones were hung to dry and used again and again before we did the weekly laundry. I spent many happy moments rocking and singing to Buddy every song I knew from church, with his tiny head tucked in the crook of my arm. I must have driven friends and family crazy with my singing. Over and over I repeated the verses until my precious baby brother fell asleep in my arms.

Buddy's birth enriched my life. He became the brightest spot of every day during the turbulent teenage years before I left the farm at age seventeen.

Tested By Fire

Ordinary events on the farm sometimes led to hazardous accidents.

I was a baby when I experienced the first incident that occurred with fire. As was often the case because of her narcolepsy, Mama fell asleep in a chair. I crawled toward the bright fire in the fireplace. My screams awoke her when I reached for the blaze and burned my little hands. Her soft brown eyes filled with tears as she told me what happened. I cannot recall the event, but it's possible my repressed memory retained the experience.

When I was six years old I suffered another burn, leaving a large scar on my upper left leg. School had already started. The cool weather required some heat. Earlier in the day a fire burned in the fireplace, leaving live coals piled against the andirons. As I leaned against the loosely attached board above the fireplace that served as a make-shift mantle, it came down, and with it I was thrown into the red-hot coals.

I screamed with pain and Mama came running. "What's wrong? Where are you hurt?" She rubbed butter on the burned places, only succeeding in making the pain more intense. I could not bear clothing to touch my burned leg. Waiting for the place to heal, I missed school. Even though the injury was severe, I was not taken for treatment for we were without transportation and had no money to pay the doctor.

Autumn arrived early the year of the bonfire incident when I was nine years old. We had finished the evening chores and night was approaching when two young men stopped by our place. The two teenage brothers, Ozimo and Junior Mount, were visiting their sister, Naomi, called "Mutt," who lived down the road. When people visited in our community, they often dropped by to see neighbors.

"Daddy, can we build a bonfire in the open space below the front yard?" my brother Hershel asked.

"I don't see why not," Daddy answered. "There's a pile of wood near there you can burn, and you kids can pop some popcorn."

In the past, Daddy allowed the children to stand nearby and watch open fires when fallen tree limbs and brush had accumulated. No one had ever gotten hurt and we did not consider it dangerous.

We gathered closely around the fire, as the night air turned chilly. We popped corn with the long-handled screen popper, using the plentiful supply harvested in the summer. The aroma of freshly popped corn filled the air as we poured it out into a big bowl and added butter and salt. Everyone ate as much as they wanted.

The bonfire grew bigger as the large logs caught fire. We laughed and talked and were enjoying the occasion. Hershel piled on more wood and the blaze burned brighter, sending sparks up into the night sky. I was not dressed warmly enough for the fall air and felt cold. Standing with my back to the fire, I suddenly realized a spark had ignited my thin cotton dress.

One of the kids yelled, "Rita, you're on fire!" I panicked. I fled, thinking I was running toward our house and my parents for help. In reality, I headed the opposite direction, terrified.

Our visitor, Junior Mount, saw what was happening and reacted quickly. He raced toward me, caught me, and pulled me to a sudden stop by throwing me to the ground. With his bare hands he smothered the flames. Thanks to his quick action I was not harmed, but I was very embarrassed about being so careless. I should have known to stand further away from the fire.

I wanted to tell Junior how brave he was, and thank him for saving me. He was a few years older than I was and my shyness kept me from sharing my feelings with him.

Hershel ran to get our parents and they came hurrying from the house.

"Oh, Rita, are you sure you're all right?" Mama asked.

Daddy then turned to my rescuer. "Thank you, thank you, for acting so quickly," he said. "Are you sure that your hands are okay? Did you burn yourself when you put out the flames?"

"I'm fine, honestly," Junior said. "See, my hands are not burned, just a little red. It's nothing; my fingers are barely scorched at all." The young man appeared reluctant to accept any praise. I shudder to think how badly I could have been burned. In my mind, Junior Mount will always be my hero.

BRUSH ARBOR REVIVAL

I watched fascinated as the cardboard fans, with advertisements by the local funeral parlor, waved faster and faster to the beat of the preacher's voice. The breeze generated little relief from the suffocating heat. Bored with watching the fans, I tried to count the hundreds of flying insects drawn to the bright kerosene lights through wide-open windows. Jammed into packed rows, people wiped sweat that trickled down foreheads. When I thought the nights might get hotter, they did.

For a more comfortable meeting place, farmers constructed a large room-sized "brush arbor." Fresh-cut tree saplings provided corner posts that held an overhead framework of small limbs covered with leaves gathered from nearby bushes and trees. Men transported the piano and benches and placed them in the improvised sanctuary.

The evangelistic meetings were well attended, almost everyone went, even those not so religious. Mama said sadly, "Some people view the revival meeting as entertainment." But occasionally a sinner, who came to scoff, found a personal relationship with the Lord.

"Your Daddy accepted the Savior in a brush arbor meeting a few miles down the road from his family's farm," Mama told us children. People referred to him as "a good man." Daddy's standards included honesty, hard work and helping his neighbors. From his off-spring, he demanded, "Respect your elders, attend church, never use God's name in vain."

As a child I looked forward to the scheduled revival as a social event and our family seldom missed attending.

"You kids round up the cows early tonight. Got to hurry and get the milking done before meetin' time," Daddy reminded us.

I wore my Sunday shoes and my newest cotton print dress with the tiny blue flowers. Children and women dressed up for the occasion. Deacons and ministers wore pants, shirts and ties, and younger men dressed in clean overalls and white shirts.

My family arrived before the song service began. We loved to sing the old hymns and most people knew them by heart: *Leaning on the Everlasting Arms, Sweet Hour of Prayer, Just as I Am* and dozens more. We sang all the verses with enthusiasm; a few persons harmonized, while the loud country twang drowned out those who sang off-key.

When Brother Orville was asked to lead in prayer; he responded at length. Brother Bill, our minister, read the Scripture from the Holy Word of God. Members were called Brother or Sister followed by their first name. Volunteers shared their experience of faith and healing during testimonial time.

The evangelist preached powerful messages of God's love and forgiveness, and spoke for at least an hour. I lost track of the time as my eyelids grew heavy, then Mama eased my head into her lap. The invitational hymns jarred me awake near the end. As people came forward to pray on the mourner's bench, or declared they wished to accept Jesus as Savior, the drawn-out invitation continued.

Those who declared their new faith were asked to come down the aisle and tell the minister of their decision. Each church member was asked to march forward to offer the right hand of fellowship to the new believer. At the close of the scheduled revival, we met together on the riverbank for new converts to be baptized while the congregation sang, "Shall We Gather at the River."

Between meetings we kids held revival meetings of our own in a clearing of trees near our house. Fallen logs became benches and a stump our pulpit. We'd mimic the minister and tried to pray and testify like people in church. We baptized in the nearby creek. We meant no harm or disrespect by pretending to play church.

People who doubted whether new converts were "born again" were gently reprimanded, "Wait 'til we see how the person lives." Changes were sometimes subtle at first, but I remember one man instantly transformed for life from an erratic alcoholic into a dependable, loving person. I admired Christians who cared for the elderly, patiently bathing, dressing and feeding them. I noticed friends and strangers were invited to stay overnight and often heard the words, "Stay and eat dinner with us." I witnessed courageous strength during sadness, illness, and poverty.

The use of drugs did not appear in our community. Cheating was not tolerated in marriage, business deals, or everyday transactions by church members.

Church people were law abiding and God fearing. We never locked our houses, property stood unattended, and no one feared theft. Gradually, over a long period of years, things changed. However, my father's ideas about trust, had not changed before the theft of his vehicle when he was in his eighties.

Daddy no longer drove his truck and instead used a four-wheeler he called a "mule." He treasured the remaining independence the vehicle allowed. He'd roam the farm and stop at the stock ponds with his fishing pole to catch catfish for dinner. A thief stole Daddy's four-wheeler one night. He'd left the keys in the ignition. After many months, the FBI recovered the vehicle in another state and shipped it home at my father's expense. Daddy purchased a new one before it was found.

Our congregation sang "God Will Take Care of You" and

gave little thought to health, property, or life insurance. That explained my surprise years later when the family met to plan my father's funeral, and the director said Daddy took out burial insurance when he and Mama were young. The premiums cost a few cents per week. Even with interest due, the policy paid only a tiny portion of the burial expenses. Daddy may have known families who struggled to pay for funeral expenses and wanted to protect us, his family.

Tragedies brought forth people who helped as much as they could. Wagons came through our valley collecting food, clothing, bedding, and household goods for those who lost their homes by fires or storms. Everyone gave something; canned goods, quilts, pillows, cooking utensils, dishes and clothing, no gift was too small when the family had lost everything.

People in our community were not perfect. However, if one member suffered, all suffered; if another rejoiced, we joined in thanksgiving. Surrounded by friends and neighbors, I felt loved.

Epilogue

The truths taught in those bush arbor meetings guide my life, to give me strength and hope for the future. When I hear of lives in turmoil, filled with rage and despair, my thoughts return to those days of innocence when people reached out to care for one another.

The Graveyard

The little country graveyard on the gently sloping hillside provides a peaceful oasis for a final resting place. Birds sing and flit about in the trees, leaves move in a gentle breeze, and in the distance the low mooing of cows can be heard from the nearby pasture.

So many stories—if we only knew—of people who lie buried there: an adorable baby girl who left heartbroken parents, a young father shot by his own brother, the mother who died when her youngest child was small, leaving a houseful of children who needed her. These stories of my relatives were handed down to me.

The graveyard presented a fascinating spot on our farm. W.W. Scroggin owned the land before he sold the property to my grandfather, George Washington Chandler in 1902. My youngest brother, Lewis, holds the records that show an acre of land was deeded for the cemetery before my relatives bought the farm.

Early in my life, someone said three mounds surrounded by a rectangular wall were the original graves. The enclosure, constructed of carefully fitted rocks built without mortar, stands three feet high and eighteen inches wide. I thought the people buried there were Indians. No headstones identified the persons, but my sister-in-law, Gay Stover Miller informed me one of her ancestors, "James Madison Scroggin, my great, great grandfather, lies buried in one of the graves."

The wall provided space to sit or walk. As children we ran

around and around the top, chasing one another. We gathered hickory nuts from the nearby trees, cracking them open and eating the kernels.

Rocks used as gravestones mark many of the older graves. The newer ones have regular tombstones containing data with names, births, and deaths. Some carry heartbreaking messages about the loss of a loved one: spouse, parent, friend, or child.

We never considered the graveyard a morbid place. We felt completely at ease playing under the large shade trees that grew there. In the summertime, after the chores were finished, we played during the long evenings when twilight gradually faded into night. More often, we kids met there during the day when we were free from working in the fields.

One evening when darkness descended, I recognized our neighbors as they approached our house that led past the cemetery. I decided to pull a prank on them, so I cut across the field and hid behind one of the gravestones. When Ethel Scoggins and her daughter, Emma Jean, came abreast of the cemetery, I tried to imagine how a really scary noise might sound, and did my best imitation. The loud ghostly groan reverberated above the silence of the gravestones. I followed with another long moan, gradually increasing in volume.

Ethel stopped in her tracks and grabbed her daughter. "Oh, my goodness, did you hear that noise?" she demanded. About that time I gave another sorrowful wail, louder and with greater feeling.

This time Ethel acted really scared, "That's groaning, Emma Jean. Oh, my god, let's get out of here!" And they took off running while I held my sides laughing.

Ethel had always spun ghost's tales to the children when we visited in the failing light as darkness approached. We never knew whether to believe her or not. I thought she should experience a true tale she could share.

Instead, the unpredictable happened. The two must have agreed never to disclose what they heard in the graveyard. Emma Jean did not tell, either, for I never heard one word about their experience. I never told anyone what I had done, not even my own family. I thought they might not understand why a normally "good little kid" would pull such a stunt and Daddy or Mama may have "spanked me good."

In 1991, my son Bob and his family came to Arkansas to visit while we were there. Bob and I went to the graveyard and he took his video camera along. He recorded the stories as I told him about the enclosed graves and how we loved to play there. As I talked, I climbed on the wall and started running around on top of the enclosure. Bob was delighted and told his grandparents, "For a few moments I had a glimpse of my mom when she was a little girl growing up in Arkansas."

TAKE COVER

———◆·◇·◆———

M y parents' faces betrayed their attempt to stay calm when funnel clouds appeared on the horizon. I thought about the danger as Mama and Daddy rushed to protect me and my siblings. When lightning flashed against a dark sky, Mama yelled for us kids to come inside, lie down on the feather bed and stay away from the windows. Lightning could strike you dead.

I don't know why my mother thought the feather bed offered any protection. Perhaps feathers were a poor conductor of electricity and my mother thought if we were blown away on top of the feather bed, we might survive. Our house, a flimsy shelter built without a storm cellar, afforded little protection.

One day our house seemed directly in the path of a suspicious-looking, rapidly approaching storm. Daddy ran into the house yelling for Mama to get the kids and run for a nearby culvert, a small cement bridge with strong supports. We had started for the door when the storm hit with a loud bang. Mama and Daddy managed to hold the door closed until the storm passed over. We thanked God that our house remained intact.

After I grew up and moved away from the south, I no longer searched the sky for danger signs. However, my concerns returned when I visited my family. In 1988 those fears surfaced during a wedding shower for my brother's youngest daughter.

My husband and I planned our visit to coincide with my niece Crystal's wedding festivities. The women at the small white church, where family members had worshiped for five generations, planned a wedding shower.

The day proved warm for late November, a cause of alarm for my husband who said, "The weather feels too warm to be normal." His anxiety made me uneasy.

As evening approached and the women arrived for the occasion, dark clouds hovered on the horizon. The bride shared my apprehensions and paced back and forth as she peered out the windows. The church reception hall filled with guests bearing beautifully wrapped gifts. The sky grew darker and lightning zigzagged in the distance.

My mind raced back to a night in 1938, when a tornado threatened our lives and cut a wide swath of destruction. I glanced at the older ladies and wondered if they were reliving that day along with me. I found myself recalling the details.

Our twin cousins, Ellen and Helen Griswood, had spent the night at our house when the tornado hit. Earlier that evening the neighbor's children, Harold and Emma Jean, came to play. Before bedtime, we played a game called "ante over." We threw a large rubber ball over the house and when the kids on the other side caught the ball, they raced to tag everyone before we changed sides.

The tranquil scene gave no hint of impending danger. As darkness fell, the sky looked completely clear with just a little lightning far off in the distance.

During the night while we slept the tornado struck. The Baptist and Methodist churches were completely destroyed, along with several houses. Homer and Girlie Stracner's house was blown away with them and their infant daughter inside. A frantic search rescued the parents from the debris. They found their baby unharmed on the bank of a nearby creek, lying on her mattress.

Adults cried with joy and hugged one another. No one died and injuries were minor.

Now I was doubly afraid for we were sitting in the exact location where the original church building had once stood.

Crystal had barely started to unwrap her gifts when a loud knock on the door startled us. Our cousin Zeke yelled, "Take cover! A tornado is heading our way!"

Gifts lying in tissue paper and bright ribbon were tossed aside. Unopened presents were abandoned on the table. Women scattered in every direction, disregarding the warnings to take cover, given for tornado danger. Everyone raced to cars and headed for home to be with their families. I rode with the frantic bride in her mom's car. The sky was black with brilliant flashes of lightning. "Mother, drive faster," Crystal kept repeating. Gay was already driving much too fast in pouring rain on narrow country roads.

Arriving home, the bride no longer thought about wedding gifts, but rather whether we would survive the night. Crystal herded all of the family into the hallways and handed out pillows to protect our heads. For added protection, she hauled heavy mattresses from beds to pad the walls.

My sister-in-law frantically dialed Mama and Daddy, but the party line continued busy. She rang the operator. "This is an emergency. I must reach my relatives. A tornado is headed our way." When my parents answered the phone she asked that they and my husband hurry to my brother's house.

Bill arrived immediately, but Mama and Daddy took their time. The wind and rain pelted the house in huge gusts by the time they arrived. Daddy had been watching one of his favorite programs—a wrestling match on TV. As he and Mama entered Lewis' house, my father grumbled, "All these precautions are nonsense."

My father's attitude had changed completely since the days he tried desperately to protect his young children. Perhaps dying by tornado appeared an easier exit than becoming increasingly decrepit and dependent. However, I think his philosophy shaped his response. "Why should I worry? I've lived a long time and never been blown away in a storm."

He and Mama settled into chairs and while everyone else shook with fear, Daddy asked, "Anyone care if I finish watching the fight on TV?"

In the midst of a quiet moment that often precedes a touch-down, a sudden whirling noise overhead terrified us. We thought we were headed for destruction, but found that my sister-in-law had switched on the ceiling fan. Amid nervous laughter, I asked, "Good heavens, woman, you trying to scare us all to death?"

"I'm sorry," Gay giggled, "but I'm terribly warm!"

Her mother groaned. "You might try removing your jacket."

We kept the radio tuned to the local station and were shocked by how many areas were being hit. The minutes ticked slowly by and at last the all clear sounded. The tornadoes veered away from our valley, but the next day news of several deaths and wide-spread destruction filtered back from out-lying communities.

Later that evening the somber bride and jittery family members returned to the church. A few hardy souls joined us as Crystal finished opening her gifts.

As her wedding day approached, we repeatedly checked the weather forecast. The day dawned clear and cold with blue skies and sunshine. The radiant bride marched serenely down the aisle on the arm of her father. The joy of the occasion erased all thoughts of tornadoes.

THE LEGACY OF POVERTY

I knew poverty first-hand during my growing-up years. My family lived in a shack with my father striving to provide for the six of us. I never received a bicycle, skates, or ready-made-store-bought clothes. We could not afford a stick of hard candy or an ice cream cone, treats I occasionally glimpsed other kids enjoying. We never celebrated birthdays and I never received gifts. I did not suffer alone; many of our neighbors bore the same problems. I noted pain in the soft brown eyes of my mother when I asked for things she could not buy.

The state of the economy ushered in drastic steps taken by the government to ease the problem. The WPA (Works Progress Administration), initiated by President Franklin D. Roosevelt, hired men desperate for work to support their families. Several people in our small community found employment with the agency.

Widespread improvements were made to country roads in our rural area. Workers built small bridges over streams and graded roads, while placing gravel on steep hillside roads to keep cars from sliding off in wet or snowy weather. Large scale improvements were made in other parts of the United States.

Hard-working farmers watched as some WPA workmen would lean on their shovels and laugh, instead of work. Some disparagingly hailed the WPA program to mean "We Play Around" or "We Putter Around." Envy may have kept people recounting the jokes years after the jobs ceased. Many workers expressed pride in accomplishments that still stand.

Because of their income, men who worked for the WPA Program spent money on themselves and their families. They were employed when jobs and cash were extremely rare. My father's older brother, Uncle Baxter, worked on such a crew.

On one project, a truckload of men that included my uncle passed our house every day. The workers packed wonderful items in their daily lunches: store-bought "light bread" filled with lunchmeat, cheese or peanut butter. Uncle Baxter told my folks that large portions of food were wasted every day. He volunteered to gather up the partly eaten sandwiches, fruit, and cookies, placed in a bag to toss out when the truck returned by our house at the end of the day. These scraps were meant to feed pigs, dogs, and chickens, but mama carefully sorted out the food from the bag and saved some for us to eat. Food that had landed on the ground was carefully inspected and separated. She wanted us to enjoy treats that we could not afford. Shame caused embarrassment. She cautioned us, "Don't tell anyone we ate these scraps."

I'd been known to share information my family preferred to keep confidential. In this case, I never confessed eating the food as long as Mama lived. We rarely suffered from hunger, but we longed for store-bought treats others enjoyed.

Some neighbors suffered even more than we did. We knew of at least one family who applied for welfare. My folks called such a program "being on relief." My parents would never ask for help. "Welfare is for people who are really bad off." During the middle of winter our destitute friends received a food allotment of a large sack of green cabbages. They urged my folks to accept some rather than "having them go to waste." "After all," they told us, "there is more than we could possibly ever use." I think the idea of food going to waste persuaded my parents to finally accept cabbages.

Many months had passed since we'd eaten fresh vegetables or fruits. Mama made coleslaw and cooked cabbages with ham hocks. We enjoyed the addition to our diet which consisted mostly of dried beans, fried potatoes, cornbread and salt pork.

The Depression era was a most difficult time for my parents. Any wasteful use of hard-earned money threw my father into a state of despair. Daddy scrutinized each request for grocery items written by Mama.

One day when I was nine years old, Daddy went into town and returned with a 100-pound sack of flour—a cash purchase, and a necessary one. We did not grow wheat. He unloaded the flour and left it leaning against a post on our front porch. A pig escaped its pen, grabbed the sack and ripped open the bag, spilling the contents onto the ground.

My father yelled at Mama, "Jewell, why didn't you take care of the flour? We don't have money to buy another sack!"

I wondered why he left the heavy sack on the front porch instead of taking it into the house. Loud angry voices punctuated the quiet of our little home as my parents shouted at one another. I tried not to hear the awful words. I hated the quarrel and the poverty that caused a sack of flour to be more important than Mama's feelings. The unjust criticism brought tears to Mama's eyes and I longed for parents who only spoke kind words to one another.

I was too young to understand that stress often causes outbursts of anger and frustration, but I did realize that I was helpless to change the situation. As I entered my teenage years, I determined to escape the poverty by leaving the farm immediately after high school graduation.

COME TO THE WATER

The summer I turned eleven, our family scanned the blue skies day after day looking for rain clouds.

"If we don't get rain soon, our well may run completely dry," Mama said.

"Don't waste a drop!" Daddy warned us, "water is getting mighty precious around here."

Because of the shortage of water in the drilled wells near our houses, my cousin Sybil, along with her twin sisters, Helen and Ellen, were sent down to the creek to wash clothes. I'd been playing at their house, so I went along with them. The water in the hand-dug well, located alongside the creek, remained high. The well measured about four feet across, with walls built of rock and cement. The water appeared only a few feet below.

"Get the tubs set up to draw water from the well." Sybil, older than us, ordered us to help.

We used a bucket tied to a rope to fill two large washtubs, one for washing the clothes and one for rinsing. When we finished filling the tubs she told us to sort the clothing into piles of light and dark. "Got to wash the white before the colored ones."

She washed the clothes on a scrub board and rubbed them with the lye soap her mother made with fat saved during hog butchering. The soap, though hard on the hands, cleaned fairly well.

As Sybil finished scrubbing each piece of laundry, she squeezed out the sudsy water, and tossed it into the rinse tub. The twins and I pushed the article up and down before wringing out by hand. We then hung the clothing on a line fastened between two trees. As we finished the washing, Helen and Ellen emptied the tubs and placed the bar of soap and scrub board in the sun to dry. The twins then looked around for something to do.

They went over to the well, climbed over the curbing and down into the opening, circling the edges as they found ledges to place their feet.

"Come on, Rita," they teased me. "Don't be such a fraidy cat!" It looked easy, but my fears made me hesitant. I was not as agile as the twins, and should never have accepted the dare.

Crawling over the curb and hanging onto the edges, I climbed down inside the well. Suddenly my feet slipped on the damp rocks. I grabbed tightly to the top rim and held on, while scrambling for firmer footing. I could have drowned. Had I fallen, rescue appeared impossible. By the time help arrived, my body would probably have been at the bottom.

Instantly, the words spoken by the evangelist the previous night during revival meeting came to my mind. "If you should die today, where will you spend eternity?" I hurriedly climbed out and told no one of my narrow escape.

As Sybil completed her tasks she caught sight of the twins and demanded they quit that nonsense and behave themselves.

I thought about the messages I'd heard daily about my need to accept Christ as Lord of my life. Seeking to know more, I'd been reading in the Gospel of John. The story of the woman at the well intrigued me. "Mama," I said, "What is the water of life?" She tried to explain her understanding of the Scripture, but I could not grasp the meaning. I was convinced I needed a Savior, but my prayers seemed worthless.

During revival meetings we stayed up much later than usual. "We all need a good nap before church tonight," Sybil said. "Let's go to Grandma Griswood's old house. We can rest during the hottest part of the afternoon while the clothes dry in the sun."

In a nearby field stood the abandoned house where my great grandparents once lived. We found an old quilt in a bedroom and spread it on the bare wooden floor. My friends soon slept.

I looked around for something to read and saw a stack of dusty books piled in the corner. The books once belonged to my Great Grandfather Griswood, who had been a minister at the local Mt. Pleasant Missionary Baptist church.

I picked up a book and opened it at random. In bold-faced type a title jumped out at me: "My Spirit Shall Not Always Strive With Man." Hurriedly, I closed the book as if it were on fire and replaced it in the corner. The Holy Spirit spoke to me as surely as a voice speaking aloud. "Don't turn away. Listen to My Voice." The convicting power of the Holy Spirit persuaded me I needed to make a decision to accept Christ as Lord.

Discouraged by my lack of understanding of the Bible and trying to pray, I knelt in my bedroom later that summer. I did not know that Jesus had been waiting for me to acknowledge my sins, and that He alone could wash and make me clean.

"Lord," I said, "I'm a sinner and need to be saved. I've been trying to get good enough to be a Christian, but I cannot. You'll just have to take me as I am." With tears streaming down my cheeks, I thanked Him as I realized He heard my prayer and took away my guilt.

His promise of the Living Water then made perfect sense to me. I drank deeply from the Well that never would run dry.

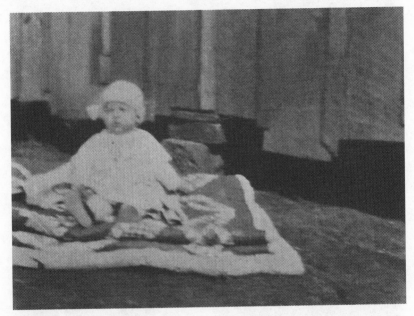

My baby photo. 1928
I've often wondered what the circumstances were for our poor
family to have any photos.

"Looking across the fields lined by trees, my thoughts transport me back to the days I walked along this same road to catch the school bus every weekday, and early mornings when I walked over the hill to the small white church for Sunday school and church."

"As we climb the hill, the farmhouse comes into view."

Our family photo before Buddy (Lewis) was born.   1929
"You might never guess from the picture that we lived in poverty, or that all of my family went barefoot in the summer to save our shoes for church."

My siblings and I. Loretta, Hershel, Opal, Lewis ~1939

Me (2nd born), Daddy (A.D.), Mama (Jewell), Hershel (1st born), Lewis (4th born), Opal (3rd born)   ~1941

Lewis, Opal, Loretta, Hershel, Mama, Daddy   ~1949

Family of Daniel Aulden & Minnie Griswood Miller.   ~1910
Daddy (A.D. Miller) age 6, is center photograph standing between
his father and mother. Wearing a white shirt, suspenders and
barefoot, he later shouldered responsibility as the man of the
house at age 17 upon the death of his father in 1921.

Daddy's father and mother ~1919
Daniel Aulden Miller & Minnie Griswood Miller

"At the close of the scheduled revival, we met together at the riverbank for new converts to be baptized while the congregation sang, "Shall we gather at the river?"

Our small battery operated radio was kept in the bookcase that served as a desk, bookshelf, and a place for important papers.

"We finally settled on a small tree that would fit on top of the desk section of the cherished bookcase made by Great Grandfather William Henry Miller."

John 4:10

"I'd been reading in the Gospel of John... the story of the woman at the well intrigued me. "Mama," I said, "What is the water of life?"

Daddy continued curing hams late into his life.   1977
"Hams were salted, seasoned, and hung in the smokehouse to be cured with slow-burning hickory wood."

Audrey Opal Mae Belle Spier
"She displayed a unique vitality and enjoyment of life that made me want to be like her."

Daddy was proud to get the most out of his investments, including this 2nd hand tractor purchased in 1942 , still running in 1982.

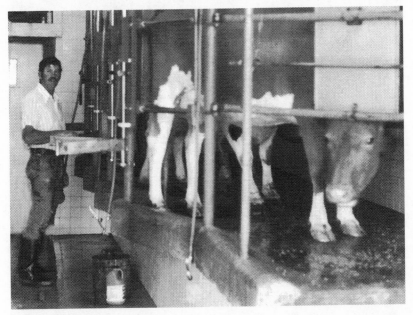

Lewis in the milk barn.   1977

"In later years Lewis took over the dairy business and both he and Daddy ran huge chicken houses that held 12,000 birds each."

Daddy tending to the chickens making one of several daily inspection walks through the house.

"Although Hershel's letters were censored, he was able to tell us that he was serving on an aircraft carrier, The Bismarck Sea."

"A news flash came over her radio while they were at my aunt's house. His aircraft carrier, The Bismarck Sea, had gone down."

"On February 21, 1945, the USS Bismarck Sea was the last US Navy aircraft carrier to be lost to enemy action during World War II. 605 officers and men of the 923 crew members were rescued, many picked up by destroyer escorts, the same type of ship that my husband served on during World War II."

Commencement 1945

"Daddy and Mama did not attend my graduation; I rode with other graduates and their relatives on the school bus. Daddy refused to discuss the occasion, so Mama stayed home with him."

Murleen, Loretta, Beth ~1946

My friends and I left our families in Arkansas and headed off to Los Angeles, California when given the opportunity to transfer there while working for Western Union. Beth, remained my dearest friend during her lifetime. I keep in touch with Murleen who continues to live in Arkansas.

Bill & I on our wedding day in Pasadena. I bought my dress off a sale rack for less than $20. September 11, 1948

"For our simple wedding I selected a full skirted gown of white satin with sweetheart neckline and fitted bodice."

"Cousin Bob Spier, my only family member in attendance, walked me down the aisle."

Dressed for church, note the stylish clothing compared to my former life on the farm.

I experienced a different life after leaving the farm for the West Coast where I met my husband, Bill. ~1948

Enjoying my "modern" kitchen just a few years after loading wood into the stove at the farm.

This photo of the farm house being built from recycled lumber is dated January 17. It was taken before the siding was added and the porch cement poured in 1949. Made to look like brick, asphalt siding was sometimes applied to cover deteriorating walls of older homes.

"I had dreamed and yearned for a nice house for my parents all my life. Now for me, the terrible fact emerged that my desire would never be fulfilled. I knew in my heart that Daddy would never build another house."

Arthur Daniel (A.D.) Miller, Daddy

"I never heard him complain. He was so intent on providing essentials, he seemed to have no idea that his children had unmet emotional needs."

Bill and I drove to the farm, my first visit after we married. Bill enjoyed photography and documented many scenes that trip. September 1949

My family with visiting cousins.   September 1949

He grew up too fast while I was away. **September 1949**

"I always knew I was loved by Lewis."

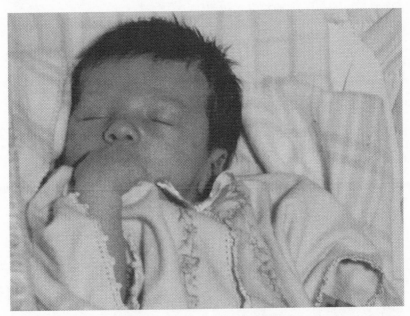

First born son, Charles **1951**

"I'll always remember that first trip carrying Charlie to the farm..."

In this picture my baby brother towers over me.   ~1958
We bought our first house in 1952 for $10,250.
"When Bill and I lived in the first house we purchased in Monterey
Park, California, Lewis came to visit."

"A large steel cable hanging from
one of the trees provided a swing
for the children... As children, we
drew it back as far as possible, and
taking a running leap, swung high
in the air."

The power lines cross the street to avoid the trees today.
"Took God over a hundred years to grow them trees. Can't see ruining 'em for an electric line!"

"...he clutched the steering wheel of an all-terrain vehicle, his beloved four-wheeler, as he slowly canvassed the well-worn paths of the farm, sometimes carrying a fishing pole to the nearest stream or pond."

A.D. Miller (21) & Jewell Chandler (19).   1924
Less than a year before they married on 12/25/1924.

Daddy and Mama's 60th wedding anniversary. Married for over
70 years, both lived into their nineties.   1984
"...a quirk of nature added irony to life's story when my father became
quite bald at an early age for the remainder of his life."

Me with siblings. Opal, Lewis, Loretta, Hershel

Mama and Daddy   1977
"Mama went to the fields to help with the backbreaking work. Once when I complained about being tired, Mama replied, 'Oh, my, you don't even know what the word means!'"

Daddy enjoyed visitin' and so did I. Some of those talks and recordings helped me to preserve these stories. Daddy always said about himself, "I did the very best I knew how."

FREE FOR THE EFFORT

Early one hot scorching August morning, Daddy hiked to the back pasture to check on a cow due to freshen. When he returned he told my mother we had a new baby calf. "Prettiest little thing," he said, "Heifer, too."

"Oh, by the way, Rita," he said, "The blackberries are goodn' ripe. You and Opal should go pickin'." When Daddy suggested we go, it sounded like an order.

"Okay," I replied, "hadn't planned on doing nothin' special today anyways."

"You girls wear those old pants and the shirts with the long sleeves, and don't fergit your sunbonnets," Mama said. She repeated the same instructions every time we picked blackberries. "Rub real good with kerosene to keep off the chiggers."

Opal and I dressed in old clothing and rubbed kerosene on our ankles, wrists, and all around our waistlines where the chiggers usually clung. We knew we'd come home covered with bites. Didn't matter what we did, they were always there. Trouble was, the pesky bugs, abundant in our area, were so tiny we never knew they were on us until it seemed like they burrowed into the skin and we started itching.

Opal and I stopped by the barn for a piece of rope to tie around our waists. By hanging the lard buckets on the rope we'd have both hands free to pick berries.

We took the toe-path through the meadow, glad that the sun

had dried the dew. Our collie dog, Carlo, ran along beside us, eager for a walk. We stopped a minute by the creek to watch the small fish dart in and out of the shadows in the shallow water. The path meandered through the woods, and as we followed it, we looked for crooked sticks to use for pulling the berries and vines toward us.

"Here's some good ones," I said, picking up two narrow sticks with pointed forks on the end.

When we arrived at the cow pasture, our herd and big bull grazed peacefully in the distance. We carefully crawled between the strands of barbed wire fence. Wild blackberry vines grew along the fence rows amid dense brush uncut for years. Beneath the tall, thorny vines lay large clusters of ripe, juicy fruit. We tried to avoid the stickers that caught our hands and clothing.

"Oh, boy, just look at these berries!" I called. We picked quickly, eating the largest, ripest ones and placing the rest in the containers. Our tongues, lips, and fingers were soon stained a bright purple-pink.

"Shouldn't take very long to fill our buckets here," I said. "Nicest blackberries I've ever seen, probably 'cause of all the rain this spring." Opal ran along from one bush to another, picking wherever the berries were easily visible.

We'd been picking about a half-hour when we heard wild, angry bellowing coming from the direction our herd grazed. The cries grew louder and closer.

"Something's wrong. Let's run!" I urged Opal. We barely made it over the top of the fence as our bull charged through the trees and into the meadow. He continued to bellow and paw the ground near the spot where we had stood.

"We'll not go back in there," I told Opal. "Let's try picking on the outside of the fence further down."

Opal, ten years old, and younger than I, looked scared. "What's wrong with that silly, old bull?" she asked.

"Don't know. Never seen him act like that before. Guess the fence will hold him inside. Come on, let's get out of his sight!" We hurried along, walking behind some bushes growing near the fence row.

We walked carefully, realizing that snakes sometimes hid in the dense growth. I was fearful my hand or foot might touch a cold, slithery creature. I stopped to pick where plentiful fruit hung from tall vines when I heard a faint rustle of leaves and caught a glimpse of the enemy near my feet. Horrified, I screamed for our dog,

"Carlo, Carlo, come!" I pointed, "Sic 'em, sic 'em, sic 'em, atta' boy!" Carlo grabbed the snake in his strong white teeth, shaking it furiously from side to side. He then placed it before me. I saw my mistake. "Oh, look, Opal, it's only a kingsnake!" I exclaimed.

"A kingsnake won't hurt anyone!" Opal said. "They kill poisonous snakes! Remember last summer when we saw one swallowing a rattlesnake."

"But I didn't know what kind it was," I moaned, really sorry I had been so eager to have it killed.

We resumed picking, wanting to fill the containers. "These darn sweat-bees are starting to sting. Let's hurry and finish so we can go home." Opal agreed, so we stopped eating and worked harder, bending down low to find the nicest berries underneath the thorny green vines. We soon filled the buckets. Now, hot and tired we left for home, taking the shortest route, eager to remove the old clothing and cool off.

"Oh, what nice blackberries," Mama said as she made the crust for the blackberry cobbler. The aroma of berries cooking with sugar soon filled our small house.

"Look, Arthur, what we have for supper," Mama said, bringing the large pan to the table, with the rich, purple juice boiling up through the crust. She served us large portions in dessert bowls and poured thick, sweet cream over the top.

"Boy, oh, boy, this is sure lip-smacking good," Daddy said, smiling at us. "Bet you found it easy to get the berries this year."

"Not 'specially," I replied, "Our old bull chased us."

"You must be joking," Daddy said, shaking his head.

"No, Daddy, the bull really did chase us," Opal said.

"Oh, my, you girls have a wild imagination. That old bull wouldn't hurt a fly!" he declared, seeming to dismiss the thought. We knew it was best not to argue with Daddy. No one in our household ever did.

Mama continued to brag about our efforts bringing me back to the present. "They got lots of berries," Mama said. "Had enough to make cobbler and blackberry jam. We'll have some for breakfast on hot, buttered biscuits straight from the oven!"

I knew the truth regardless of what Daddy thought. The bull could easily have hurt us had we not escaped when we did. Daddy would have warned us to stay far away from the herd had he thought the bull dangerous. Perhaps entering the territory occupied by the new calf had triggered the loud demonstration of outrage.

I made a mental note: Parents can be wrong even when they insist they are right.

DAIRY FARMER'S DAUGHTER

As far back as I can remember our family raised dairy cattle. During the 1930's, we milked by hand and "stripped down" the cow's bag to the last few drops. We carried the milk in large buckets to the cream separator for processing. The large machine separated the cream from the raw milk. Skim milk poured from one spout and cream from another. Mama then stored the cream in metal cans in cool troughs of water until sold.

The metal parts of the cream separator included dozens of small discs. We meticulously washed each part in hot, soapy water and scalded the pieces with boiling water from an iron teakettle. Daddy carefully monitored sanitary conditions so cream taken to market tested okay for bacteria count and grade. The best grade brought the highest price.

During Daddy's earliest years of dairy farming, he did not sell milk. He only sold the cream and fed skim milk to the pigs, calves, and cats. We did not consider it "rich" enough to drink. We kept whatever whole milk we needed for personal use and saved cream for churning into butter. Occasionally a five-gallon can of cream became bitter, a sign that the cream had started to sour. No longer suitable for selling, we fed that cream to the pigs.

We used an old-fashioned crock for churning butter. The procedure seemed to take hours for the butter to "come." When small pieces of butter floated in the milk the process was near completion. We drank the creamy buttermilk and ate it with the cornbread Mama baked. We also used buttermilk for making bread. If we accumulated too much on hand or it turned too sour, we fed it to the hogs.

Later Daddy sold whole milk to the cheese plant at Morrilton. We no longer used the cream separator. We set aside milk needed for our personal use. Mama waited for the milk to cool, skimming the thick cream from the top. She placed the cream in a large glass container on the warming shelf of the wood burning stove. A few days later the cream was sour enough to churn.

As our herd of cattle increased, changes in the dairy farming occurred. The early operations in dairy farming contrasted greatly with the modern equipment used later: automatic milking machines, stainless steel holding tanks, refrigeration equipment and periodic checking to meet health standards.

During my childhood dozens of cats roamed constantly underfoot. We tried to keep them from coming inside of the house, although they were free to wander the barn, smokehouse, and outbuildings. Cats were not allowed in the house where they would search for food. We had no refrigerator. We left food on the table covered by a cloth or placed in the wood stove oven for storage. Our iron skillets were seasoned from years of deep-frying and covered with lids instead of being washed. We left food not eaten inside the skillet to be continually re-cooked to keep from spoiling. We did not store food in the kitchen cabinets, for mice invaded the kitchen.

One Saturday when we expected visitors, Mama prepared the cream to churn and placed the glass container on the warming shelf of the cook stove. As I came into the house from an outside door, a cat slipped in beside me. We had a strict rule. "If you let a cat into the house you must immediately chase it outside."

The cats on the farm were not tame. We did not pick them up

or pet them. The only way to remove one from the house was to open the door and chase the cat outside.

I grabbed a broom and started after the cat, "Git out of here, you dumb cat, you! Scat! Scat!" I ran around and around the room and the cat ran everywhere except near the open door. Finally I got too close for the cat's comfort with the broom. He leaped to the top of the stove knocking over the container of cream. The glass jar broke with a great splash onto the iron cookstove. The cream splattered over the walls, floor, cabinets, and practically everywhere.

"Mama!" I yelled, "Come and look what the cat did!" I was angry not only at myself, but also at the cat and the whole miserable situation.

The kitchen lay in shambles as we tried to wipe up the mess with rags. The water stored in the hot water compartment of the stove was long since stone cold. We had no modern cleaning agents. We used home-made lye soap.

My mother was upset. "Rita, couldn't you be a little more careful when you are chasing the cat?" However, she could see that I was near tears and she went to work helping me clean up the havoc.

"Well," she said, "I guess we'll just have to start all over again!" I knew Mama was more upset because we were expecting company.

"Mama," I said, "I'm terribly sorry. I had no idea that crazy cat would jump on top of the stove." The experience made me leery of cats lingering near the doors. I chased them away before I opened any door.

Many years later when my young daughter Sheri visited the farm, she found some adorable kittens running around the yard. She tried to catch one to pet before she had to finish her visit on the farm that day. I warned her they were not tame. She was determined to try and she managed to grab one that reacted by scratching large bleeding places on her arms. Later that day we drove her to the airport to fly home alone. During the flight she became very ill. We never knew whether her illness was related to the cat attack.

YOU'LL DO GREAT

"You'll be perfect as the Japanese lady." Miss Mavis, my homeroom teacher said, heaping praises on my potential ability to perform before the entire school.

"Your dark hair, olive skin and slender build will look authentic."

I wished to please my teacher, but I hesitated, for I had only performed in one play at our small country church. I was extremely shy and felt uncertain about being in the spotlight even for a few minutes.

Miss Mavis's enthusiastic encouragement finally convinced me. Even so, I had to keep reminding myself of her words, "Oh, yes, you'll do great!"

On the day of the performance, Miss Mavis styled my hair high on my head and fastened it in place with several large combs. She rouged my cheeks, painted my lips bright red, and dusted my face with white talcum powder. My teacher painted my eyes with a black eyebrow pencil and finished by brushing layers of black mascara on my eyelashes. I dressed in a bright blue silk kimono to complete my costume. I hardly recognized myself in the cloakroom mirror.

I was nervous about how well I would perform. At last the curtain opened. I awaited my speaking part seated on the stage with several other students. Upon hearing my cue, I walked carefully to the front of the stage in my tight-fitting garment.

Following the script I had memorized, and proceeding as rehearsed, I turned to face those on the stage, with my back to the audience. Opening my bamboo fan, I bowed very low before speaking.

Suddenly I heard hysterical laughter from the audience. Bewildered and temporarily stunned by the response, I waited for the laughter to subside before continuing. I thought my actions were perfect, but knew something had triggered the explosive outburst. Somehow I succeeded in finishing my lines.

After the performance my teacher and classmates told me, "You did a great job." But they did not make eye contact, and I felt they'd prefer discussing other subjects. The young principal, Mr. Walton, appeared uncomfortable when speaking to me about my part in the play. I noticed his face and neck turned beet red.

Finally, several days later, my friend Nina told me why the entire student body exploded in laughter. When I bowed very low with my back to the audience, the thin silk material of my kimono clung closely to every curve of my rear, exposing more of me than I knew.

My performance added unexpected entertainment to the program. The long applause rang throughout the auditorium.

Now in my eighties, the memory lingers, bringing a smile to my face and feelings of empathy for a timid teen-aged girl.

GONE WITH MY CHILDHOOD

M y favorite escape from the reality of life was to read everything I could find. We subscribed to the Kansas City Star that came through the mail once each week and carried a serial story. I could hardly wait for the day the paper would arrive for the next installment. The story went on and on, often for months on end.

Love of reading got me into trouble early in life when a neighbor gave me a stack of "True Story" magazines. The descriptive stories were totally unsuitable for a teenage girl. When my older cousin, Sybil, saw what I was reading, she persuaded me to carry them into the yard and burn them.

One day at the local auction Daddy bought a washtub that was filled with books. That is how I came to read *Robinson Crusoe*, *Mysterious Island*, and other books written for more mature readers. Later, when attending Springfield Junior High School, I checked out books, usually brought by my teacher from the public library in town. I devoured the stories.

When I was older I discovered the library located near Morrilton High School and used my lunch hour to read and check out books. I then stayed up late at night reading by the kerosene light after all my family was fast asleep.

My time for reading was very limited. I helped in the fields after coming home from school, working as long as daylight. The field work was followed by our nightly chores shared by all the family; milking the cows, pumping water, feeding the calves, slopping the hogs, carrying in wood, and washing the dishes.

After the daily work was finished, I could hardly wait to begin reading. I waded into huge books. *Gone with the Wind* was one of them. I lived out each vivid scene in my imagination. The book was made into a movie when I was in high school and featured at the local theater. The only movies I had ever seen were the flickering black and white movies shown on small screens at the local junior high school. More than anything in the world I wanted to see *Gone with the Wind*.

One day I heard the neighbors talking about a trip to see the movie. My cousin Thurman Robinson planned to take a group in his truck. "There's plenty of room and anyone can go if they want!" I ran home to tell my parents. There was just one insurmountable problem. The price of the tickets was considered very high. I did not have even one dime and no way to earn money.

I begged and cried, but Daddy said, "No! We can't spend money on such foolishness and that is final!" There was no use going to my mother, for Daddy had the final say in all matters and Mama had no money at all.

The night the neighbors rode off to see the movie was a heartbreaking time in my young life. My tears did not make the slightest difference in the outcome, but I resolved that someday I would escape from such cruel poverty. I complained bitterly about the difficulties in my life until my father would storm, "Not one more word out of you!" If I violated that order I would be spanked. I learned it was easier to obey.

Many years after I had left the poverty of my childhood, my husband, Bill took me to the movie I longed to see. By then, "going to the picture show" wasn't nearly as exciting as I had imagined it would be. As a young girl, I had never been to the theater or seen a movie in color. Though I knew I could never go back and be able to have that experience, I was grateful for Bill's loving attempt to make up for the hurt I felt so long ago.

DADDY BUYS THE FARM

Mama's parents bought the Chandler farm in the Hill Creek community, November 8, 1902 from William Wilson Scroggin, 280 acres, for $2,000.00, with one acre previously deeded for the Scroggins Cemetery. Grandma and Grandpa raised their ten children there: Nola, Viola, Hattie, Frank, Alta, Tennie, Roy, Georgia, Jewell (my mother), and Sylvia. My grandparents, along with many other settlers, came from Georgia, and the Hill Creek community was originally called the Georgia Settlement. Until my father purchased the farm, Aunt Tennie and Uncle Alex lived in the main house after Grandfather Chandler died. I was eleven years old when we moved to the big house. At the time of my grandfather's death, the farmland was in poor condition and not very valuable.

After my grandparents died and the heirs inherited the property, Daddy acquired the ownership piecemeal from Mama's siblings. My father had not planned on buying the first portion he acquired, but felt sorry for my aunt and her desperate situation.

One summer when Aunt Hattie visited from California, she approached my father, for she heard of his penny-pinching ways. "Arthur, I know you have money saved and I want you to buy my share of the farm." Daddy tried to talk her out of it. "I've got hardly no money and can't pay you what the land might be worth. Why don't you wait until later to sell?" But Hattie insisted, "I need the money. Give me whatever you can!" Daddy reluctantly agreed, but said, "I can only pay $50.00 for your share and no more."

A few years later she came by our house obviously upset, saying, "Arthur is a liar! He told me he would pay me more later! He stole my share of the farm!" Mama, the peacemaker, did not defend my father. Mustering all the righteous indignation of an angry thirteen-year-old, I yelled at my aunt, "You get out of our house. No one is going to stand here and call my father a liar!" I do not remember ever seeing her after that time.

Over time, only two portions remained outstanding. The families of the two siblings, who had died, Viola and Frank, did not wish to sell their inheritance and asked that their portion of the farm be sub-divided on the east boundary line. Their request was fulfilled on a surveyed portion of 2/10th of the property. The deed, recorded in my father's name December 22, 1938, shows the farm as 200 acres. The heirs, who earlier begged Daddy to buy their shares, wanted additional money. Daddy remained firm saying he met his agreement and did not owe anything further.

My youngest brother, Lewis, and his wife, Gay, now own the farm, and hold the records indicating Daddy paid off the original mortgage from Federal Reserve Bank, St. Louis, Missouri, in the amount of $900.00. Back taxes and interest, plus other closing costs, may have added to the total price.

Shortly after my father bought the farm, he continued to plant cotton and corn crops that depleted the soil. The back-breaking labor required extremely long hours and produced little return for his efforts. He searched for an easier method to earn money.

As Daddy's herd of cattle grew, he gradually switched to dairy farming. He changed the many acres used in row crops to hay and pastureland. Daddy spent a large part of his life, along with the help of my brother Lewis, in dairy farming. As soon as she became old enough, Lewis' daughter, Tawnia, also helped with the cattle.

In later years Lewis took over the dairy business and both he and Daddy ran huge chicken houses that held 12,000 birds each. Two rabbits placed in the chicken house hopped throughout the night and kept the flock moving and eating, resulting in heavier weight and greater profit. Trucks hauled fryers to market every seven weeks. The manure, used as fertilizer, greatly enriched the soil. Daddy said, "It would pay to raise chickens if for no other reason than for the fertilizer." His major sources of income became the dairy and fryers.

On Sunday afternoons, Daddy walked around the farm he had earned by hard labor. He loved the view: the gently sloping land with the creek that ran across the back of the property, and the large growth of trees that bordered the bottom of the steep hillside from which Hill Creek community got its name. The stream running along the base of the hill and the slant of the land to the water provided an ideal site for a dam.

Federal Agents declared a portion of the farm to be taken over by eminent domain and paid whatever they decided the value to be. My family objected to the acreage being taken for the project, but their protest went unheeded. My father was seventy-eight years old at the time. Although the title had been transferred to my brother, Daddy's center of attention remained the farm. Eleven families were forced to sell portions of their property for a dam to provide water for the city of Conway, 20 miles away.

In 1968 Daddy sold the farm to Lewis Earl, my brother who had invested his life on the place. Mama and Daddy continued living in the farmhouse until their deaths. They took an active interest in the many changes during their lifetime: the modernized dairy with automatic equipment, tractors with air conditioning and heating, and the new water system that brought "city" water to the farm. After electricity was installed in our area, Mama and Daddy enjoyed modern conveniences available to many

Americans, a refrigerator, washing machine and clothes dryer. Eventually they installed inside plumbing with running water and bathroom facilities.

Daddy earned money throughout the years. He started investing in tax-free stocks and bonds while continuing to save every penny. He once told me, "I've never eaten a hamburger at McDonald's, for it's cheaper to eat at home."

While discussing finances with my husband, Daddy said, "I do not like to spend money." And yet, several years before my father died, he started giving his money away to each of us, his children. I made him a promise, although he did not require it. I would hold the principal as long as he and Mama lived, spending only the income from the investments. Daddy also gave substantial amounts to his church, and included a sizeable contribution for building a parsonage. Even so, my parents' estate resulted in a significant amount divided equally among his four children.

The farm boy succeeded in accumulating a "nest-egg" he lacked when he married. He accomplished one of his goals of never having to ask anyone for financial help. He was an unusual farmer, having never taken a loan. Daddy was never truly free from the poverty our family experienced during the Great Depression.

Years after I left the farm, and after he had the financial resources to improve his and mamma's life at home, he chose to continue to save and exercised extreme thriftiness the rest of his life.

UNFULFILLED EXPECTATIONS

"Mama, why won't Daddy buy any new furniture?" Silly question. I knew the answer by heart. "We can't afford to buy new things." We made do or did without.

I wanted to live in a dream world. In the books I read, characters owned large houses filled with magnificent furnishings. But families in our community struggled with poverty. Only a few enjoyed a higher standard, but that did not keep me from wishing.

Our worn furniture never changed during my growing-up years. As the years marched along, my hope of getting anything different died. When Daddy and Mama were first married, they bought two used items for their bedroom: a dresser with an attached mirror, and an iron bedstead. After seventy-one years of marriage, the pieces remained.

Our beds, with iron frames and wooden slats, featured feather beds handed down from older generations. My parents never purchased chests of drawers, sofas, or easy chairs. Early memories included unfinished, straight-backed chairs, a battered wooden kitchen table, and an old iron cook stove.

Our house had a "bookcase" built by my father's grandfather. Although it was called a bookcase, it did not look like one. The base, constructed similar to a small table fitted with slender legs, had a small front drawer. The top portion, installed upon the base, had several cubby hole shelves which held an odd assortment—scissors, hair clippers, a shaving mug, kitchen matches, writing paper, pencils, notebooks with old records, a book-keeping ledger, and a Bible. Daddy conveniently placed a container of snuff on the bottom shelf.

Our dishes were a hodgepodge of patterns, shapes, and sizes, our silverware and cookware equally mismatched. Snuff glasses made plentiful drinking containers. Pieces of worn-out clothing served as dishrags and towels. Mama bought yardage for bath towels and hemmed the pieces on the pedal sewing machine. We emptied hundred-pound sacks that originally held flour, sugar, or feed for the livestock for material for sheets and pillowcases. Our early houses had bare windows unadorned by curtains or shades.

Rural areas lacked electricity. Therefore, we had no refrigerator, electric lights, or appliances. Telephones were not available. We rejoiced when we finally got a battery radio, which Daddy cautioned us to use mostly for news broadcasts. We listened to the *Grand Ole Opry* on Saturday nights and sometimes heard the *Old Fashioned Revival Hour* broadcast from Long Beach, California, featuring Charles R. Fuller. He later established the Fuller Seminary in Pasadena, California, from which Julie, our daughter-in-law, graduated.

We had no running water, and therefore no indoor toilet, bathtub, or sinks. We heated all hot water on the iron cook stove fueled by chopped wood kept in a firebox. We washed dishes in a dishpan by hand, rinsed them in another container, and dried them with a cloth. We bathed in a washtub.

We washed clothes on a scrub board in the yard; white clothing boiled in the iron wash pot. We hung our laundry on a clothesline to dry. When we ran out of line and clothes pins, we spread the "washin'" on nearby bushes or fences.

When I was in Junior High School, Daddy announced, "We've

decided we will improve the looks of our house by wallpapering one of the bedrooms."

"Rita, you're good at math," Daddy said. "You figure the number of rolls of wallpaper we'll need." We chose a floral design, never realizing that matching the corners would be difficult. I filled in the order form from the Sears Roebuck catalog.

I have no idea what went wrong.

When the package arrived, we not only had enough to paper one large room, but enough for the entire house. I wanted to hide with embarrassment. We never returned anything and kept the surplus rolls.

On one occasion Daddy came home from the sales auction barn and announced, "I bought new 'rugs' for the girls' bedroom and the kitchen floor." I watched as he brought linoleum into the house and placed it on the floor. "You realize that this is not new stuff?" he asked. The flower designs were worn through to the backing.

"Daddy, how could you?" I cried. "Can't we just once buy something decent for our house?" My protests made no difference. He placed one over the bare wooden floor in the bedroom where Opal and I slept, and the other in the kitchen. The linoleum "rugs" continued in use after I graduated from high school in 1945.

MY PURPLE COAT

The rich, black loam deposited by periodic flooding of the land along the Arkansas River produces an abundant cotton crop. Since our cotton has already been harvested, my parents give me permission to "go to the bottoms" to pick cotton. My cousin, Thurman Robinson, hauls a truckload of pickers to the cotton fields and many of our neighbors go. He charges a small fee for the privilege of riding on the back of his truck.

Mama wakes me from a deep sleep, "Hurry and get ready before the truck comes by. Can't wait on anyone."

I hurriedly dress and eat the hearty breakfast of fried eggs, sausage, and milk gravy ladled over freshly baked biscuits. I'm ready in plenty of time before the truck appears. The group is in high spirits, laughing and talking, as we load on the bed of the same truck used for taking cattle to the auction barn. We anticipate the money we will earn from working in the fields.

The early morning air is cool as the wind whips hair around my face and I hug myself, trying to ward off the cold. I see some of the older women wrap their cotton sacks across their shoulders and hunker down, using the cab as a windbreak. The trip is short, 15 or 20 miles to reach the farm where we will pick cotton.

We fan out across the cotton field, each person responsible to pick two rows at a time. The cotton stalks are loaded with opened bolls, each plant resembling a small tree heavy with fruit. We toil steadily in the hot autumn sunshine, removing the white, fluffy cotton from the jagged-edged bolls. Each person pulls a long canvas sack that fits around one shoulder. We deposit the cotton into the bag as it drags along on the ground.

I am dressed in an old cotton dress and a jacket with long sleeves made of rough feed sack material. I wear a sunbonnet to shade my face, but nothing protects my bare legs and feet. The sweat bees begin to bite and sting as I swat at them. I hurry to fill my sack, bending over the long, seemingly endless rows that stretch out in the distance. When the sack becomes too heavy to pull, I take it to the scales at the edge of the field, the weighing station. The boss weighs my sack and writes down the number of pounds by my name before it is emptied into the big wagon with tall sideboards.

I take a short break at noon to eat my lunch, a couple of biscuits with slices of fried salt pork, wrapped in a piece of newspaper. I hurry to finish eating while sitting under a shade tree on my cotton sack. When the "water boy" comes with a fresh bucket of water and hands me the dipper, I drink deeply. I'll be terribly thirsty before he appears again.

When the end of the day finally arrives the driver calls "quittin' time." We finish weighing whatever cotton we have in our sacks, and stand by eagerly to see what our totals will be. I've had a good day. I'm paid 50 cents for 100 pounds, and I've picked a little over 200 pounds. Some of the workers have picked more than I have.

We are quiet as we load up for the trip home, too tired for small talk at the end of a backbreaking workday.

After several weeks, I earn nearly $27.00 (5,400 lbs). I anticipate buying a new sweater and skirt for school and hope I have enough money left over to buy material for a new dress. I need a new winter coat, for I have grown much taller, but I think Daddy might buy me one. Instead, I discover he expects me to use the money

I've earned to buy the coat I need so badly. I'd never had a new coat before, only hand-me-downs.

All during the autumn while I'm working, our neighbor, Ethel Scoggins bragged about her daughter. "Emma Jean's going to buy a purple coat. That's the color in style this year."

I'm easily influenced, and after listening to Ethel for weeks, I'm convinced that I should shop for a purple coat, too. No one; Mama, Aunt Altie, my friends, gives me advice about selecting or choosing the right style or color. In my inexperience, I fail to consider that I will be wearing the coat for the remainder of my years in high school and how tired I'll be of wearing the color purple.

The day Daddy and I leave for town in the old truck I tie my money in a handkerchief that I clutch in my hand. Mama has some final words before I leave, "You're old enough to choose your own coat. Look at the price tag and pick one that costs what you can afford." I've worked so hard to earn the money; I know I should be very careful about how it is spent.

I pass by Frank Brothers' Store where Daddy usually buys our shoes at what he thinks are discounted prices. I've heard stories of how the owner marked prices higher than he expected to get. He allows Daddy to haggle with him to get a lower price.

I want nothing to do with such dickering and head for O'Neals, known for quality clothing. There are racks and racks of purple coats being shown that season, and not many other choices. I try many styles and sizes while the clerk stands nearby complimenting me on each one. "That coat looks great on you!" I find one that seems "meant for me," enjoying the image in the mirror of myself, noting how nice the color looks with my blue eyes, dark hair and tanned complexion. "I'll take this one," I say, as I pay my money and am reassured. "You'll not be sorry." As I leave the store I see how little money I have left to buy anything else.

The coat is quality merchandise and the material does not wear out even though the styles and fashion color change the next year. I take the coat with me when I start working in Little Rock after high school graduation. My salary barely covers living expenses and I cannot afford a new coat. Finally, I've had enough of the purple color and I ask a dry cleaning establishment to dye the coat black. The heavy coat feels good during the cold weather in Arkansas.

The following year the telegraph company transfers two friends and me to the Los Angeles office. I soon find the coat too warm for wearing to work or social occasions. I donate it to the Salvation Army, hoping a homeless person will appreciate the protection during the cooler nights of winter.

FEASTING ON OUR BOUNTIFUL SUPPLY

City relatives envied our family's abundant fresh produce in the summertime and food canned in jars for winter. They appeared to have no idea about the hard labor and rough times we endured to grow our food supply, and that included butchering hogs and raising chickens for meat.

We preserved and canned fruits and vegetables to supplement our diet during the year. Mama never let anything go to waste. With help from us kids, she prepared fruits and vegetables to be eaten fresh or canned or given away. Our farm produced a wide variety of vegetables: corn, green beans, peas, turnips and turnip greens, mustard greens, tomatoes, okra, and beets. Mama and Daddy gave away sacks of vegetables to relatives and friends. Watermelons and cantaloupes grew in abundance and were shared.

Beginning in the spring, we relished the first small leaves of lettuce picked and prepared with green onions and tiny red radishes. Mama made a wilted lettuce salad, using hot bacon grease and vinegar. She added a touch of sugar for a delicious sweet-sour taste.

The making of sauerkraut from cabbage was a long process. Shredded cabbage placed in a crock with vinegar and salt was left to ferment before canning.

Processed cucumbers turned into dill pickles by a similar method. Large green cucumbers were alternated in layers with dill, followed by layers of grape leaves, all items grown on the farm. We grew dill plants that volunteered each spring. The grape leaves were gathered from a vine Grandmother Chandler planted. The ingredients were covered with a mixture of vinegar, water, and salt. After leaving the pickles to ferment, they were then taken from the container and canned.

Cousin Odusca thought Mama made the best dill pickles in the whole world. She went around munching on them when she visited during the summer. Mama also made sweet pickles and bread and butter pickles.

Our family enjoyed a wide variety of fruits. Grandfather Chandler planted a large orchard of peach trees and a few were still producing when Daddy bought the farm. We ate tree-ripened fruit fresh from the trees, sliced served with cream and sugar, and made into peach cobblers. Mama canned peaches in glass jars, covering with thick, sweet syrup. We dried whatever was left. Peaches were perishable and had to be used promptly.

In a few short years, grandfather's remaining peach trees were cut down after becoming diseased and dead. Daddy then resorted to buying peaches by the bushel when they were available and he felt we could afford them.

A couple of pear trees survived year after year and produced large, juicy pears. Mama made candied pear preserves, thick with sugar. During the autumn Daddy placed green pears in boxes of cotton seed to slowly ripen. In the winter the fruit turned yellow, soft and dripping with sweet juice that ran down our fingers and arms.

We begged Daddy to plant more fruit trees, but he never did. He said pruning, spraying, and fertilizing were too much trouble. One tree, planted during Mama's childhood, looked dead, but still produced large golden pears when we visited in 1982.

Mama cut any surplus peaches and apples into small pieces for drying. My brother Hershel carried the fruit to the tin roof of a nearby shed, placed it on a cloth, and covered with cheesecloth to protect from flies. When a dark cloud appeared on the horizon with rain imminent, he ran quickly to rescue our prized bounty.

Children picked wild blackberries, cherries, huckleberries, and mulberries. We ate persimmons in the autumn after the frost removed the leaves and touched the fruit, turning it bright yellow-orange as it ripened to a sticky treasure.

After the hard work during hot summers we looked forward to autumn and then endured icy winter weather. An extremely cold snap meant hog killing time. Pork chops, side pork and pork shoulder cuts were stored and salted down in a wooden box

Our family ground our own sausage, adding the sage and other seasonings to our liking. Mama cooked the patties, covered with grease, and sealed in glass jars. Everyone feasted on fresh spare ribs and pork chops. Mama pickled the hog's head, feet, and ears for souse and mincemeat. Hams were salted, seasoned, and hung in the smokehouse to be cured with slow-burning hickory wood.

"Cracklins" were made from trimmed fat and fried until crisp. These pieces were sometimes added to cornbread. Mama fried pork skins until crunchy and added salt to taste. Almost every part of the hog was used, including lard rendered from fat.

Peanuts grown every year were taken for granted, as long as the supply lasted. When roasted in the oven, or shelled and cooked on top of the stove, the aroma filled our house. Peanuts usually lasted until harvesting the next season's crop.

Popcorn was another favorite. We popped corn in a big covered skillet on the top of the stove, using generous amounts of butter and salt. When a fire burned in the fireplace, we held a wire corn popper over the flames.

Daddy planted several rows of popcorn every year. When our supply was depleted we did not rush out to buy more. We did without. Then we resorted to parching regular corn, roasting the dried kernels very brown and adding lots of butter and salt. Although hard to chew, it tasted good. Farmers faced many varied problems before enjoying the abundant supply of food.

Everything sounds pretty idyllic; however, the hours of work have been omitted. To paint the complete picture the hard times must be included. My friend said it very well, "The abundant food supply was all seasonal, very seasonal," and even then there were many times when we were short-changed.

During the early spring when the fruit trees were in full blossom, a hard freeze could destroy the crops. Later in the year after the garden was planted, scurrying clouds might fail to produce rain during the growing season. Since we had no irrigation or any way of watering, we watched our hopes for splendid eating die in the field. Other years produced heavy rains that continued "with no let-up in sight," washing away precious seed and leaving a muddy quagmire, failing to dry out in time to grow anything except dismally small vegetables. Finally, there were the bugs, the blight, and occasionally the withering of plants, seemingly without cause.

In between the sweet fruit, fresh-picked vegetables, and hog killing time, we ate dried beans and peas, fried potatoes and cornbread, biscuits and gravy, and we were glad to get it.

Oh, yes, we ate high on the hog during certain times of the year, but we had no refrigerators or freezers to preserve the fresh spare ribs, pork chops, or sow belly. A lovely picture of nostalgia requires little imagination when the unfinished landscape of hard times is omitted.

The difficult seasons included working in the 90 to 100

degree-plus temperatures, with humidity about equal; of walking on ground so hot it burned your bare feet, (until they got so toughened up, like my daddy's feet, that you could strike a kitchen match on the bottom). We stepped on "stickers" one couldn't avoid and then had to wait for places to fester when the splinter would shoot out along with the pus. We swatted sweat bees that stung, mosquitoes that bit, house flies that pestered you to death. It felt like chiggers burrowed deep under our skin causing us to scratch ourselves till we bled, leaving large sores.

During the noon break from work, we often fell asleep on the bare wooden floor. Other times we were so tired we wondered if we could keep chopping, hoeing, and harvesting the crops, but kept going, for it was necessary no matter what.

The bounty was there, sure it was, but "life ain't easy," Daddy would say.

The Homecoming

The Japanese attacked Pearl Harbor December 7, 1941 and the young men raced to sign up for military duty. The subject was discussed around every family dinner table, rich and poor, young and old, healthy and sick, every person in our nation was caught up in the changes brought about by World War II.

At first, no one in our family qualified for military service. Hershel had his 16th birthday just 4 days before the bombing. By his 17th birthday he was eager to join his friends who were already serving in far off places.

"But you don't need to be drafted. Farmers are considered an essential occupation. They are exempt!" My father's voice was loud.

"Who wants that? Only cowards refuse to volunteer! Why can't I go? All the guys are volunteering!"

"You're too young! Wait till you're older. I need you. The girls are no help at plowing fields or pitching hay."

"I can't wait! Once I am drafted they'll put me in the army or anyplace they want me. Please, Dad, I want to join the Navy!"

The argument had gone on for months and there was no end to it. Hershel was my brother and the nearest to me in age. At age seventeen, the signature of a parent was required before he could sign up for the Navy. My parents felt he was too young to go to war. Hersh felt that he must go, and he continued to beg at every chance. He thought that Mama could never understand. After all what did mothers know about protecting the country from the enemy? They were much too sentimental and tearful and knew nothing about fighting a war.

Eventually he wore my father down with his pleading. Very little work would be accomplished by a son who was terribly unhappy staying at home while his friends were all gone. "Okay, if you must go, I'll sign." With deep misgivings he gave his consent and the two left early the next morning for the recruiting office.

The officer in charge had instructions for the recruit. My brother must be at the station at Morrilton at 7:00 AM the following Saturday morning to leave for the induction center in Little Rock. He was given four days to finish all the details for leaving civilian life, four days of feeding the pigs and milking the cows, four days to prepare to leave all that was familiar and normal. It was barely time to walk through the quiet forest and gaze across the green pastures, barely time to say goodbye.

The leave-taking was too sudden for us all. The happiness that he thought would come with Daddy's signature was not evident. He suddenly looked sad and I thought of how everything must now appear strangely dear and heartbreakingly familiar. He looked confused, like a small boy who had gotten his way and then found that it was not really what he wanted after all.

Daddy took him to town in the old farm truck. Hershel took very little with him; clothing and toilet articles would be issued to him upon arrival at the induction center. Daddy stood on his toes to get a last glimpse of his eldest son as the bus pulled away. He had grabbed Hershel's shoulders and pulled him tightly to him at the last moment, but he did not trust himself to speak. The contribution of sending his first-born off to war must have seemed far too great.

In a few days Hersh's civilian apparel, which he had been

wearing when he left, was shipped home. Mama cried when the package arrived and she slowly unpacked the clothing, recalling how he had looked when she had kissed him goodbye.

The war went on and on. It seemed an eternity since the Japanese had bombed Pearl Harbor. We listened to all the news reports and wondered where my brother was serving and if he was safe and well. We waited eagerly for the mailman to bring the precious letters. Although Hershel's letters were censored, he was able to tell us that he was serving on an aircraft carrier, The Bismarck Sea.

My brother did not write about the war activities, if he was in dangerous areas, or his duties. He did write about his friends on the ship. One was the ship's chaplain, and he and Hersh shared similar Protestant backgrounds. They both came from small country communities and talked about the Sunday morning church services at home and the hymns they sang while growing up. The chaplain told Hershel about his wife and two children and how eager he was to have the war over so he could return home to be with them.

Hershel wrote about some large, glossy pictures that the chaplain had given him. He planned to bring them home when he came on leave. "The chaplain gave the pictures to me because I was easy to recognize in them," he wrote to us. "I'm keeping them in my locker with my other personal things and will buy an album when I get home."

The war correspondents daily gave vivid details of the horrors of war: heartbreaking stories of Japanese suicide planes that sacrificed lives of young men determined to gain the full glory of those who died for their country. We heard stories of our heroes who dove on bombs just in time to save their friends, but gave their own lives in the process.

Our small sacrifices seemed petty in comparison. Everything deemed necessary for daily living was rationed: gas, sugar, flour, clothing, shoes. Each person was issued ration books with coupons to be used in order to buy certain goods. Our lives continued much the same at home as we tried to live as normal as possible.

Then a day we would never forget—in February 1945, Mama and Daddy left to go to town. Hershel had been gone for over two years. They stopped by Aunt Altie's house for a list of grocery items to buy for her. One trip with rationed gas often served for more than one family. A news flash came over her radio while they were at my aunt's house. His aircraft carrier, The Bismarck Sea, had gone down. The casualties were high and number of survivors unknown.

I was in the kitchen and wondered why my parents were returning so suddenly, for I knew they could not have gotten back from town so soon, and then I caught a glimpse of Mother's face, crumpled by grief. I ran to them.

"What is it? What's happened? Tell me, please!"

But Mama could not talk for crying. Daddy finally got the words out. "Hershel's ship has gone down. We do not know if he is dead or alive."

"Oh, God, no!" I prayed, bargained, petitioned, demanded, pleaded, "Father in Heaven, please let him be alive, please God!"

A whole week went by with no word, no terrible message from the War Department. No message as to whether Hershel had survived. The days crept sorrowfully by. We went about our usual farm tasks. The cows had to be milked, the pigs slopped, the fields tended.

And then one day by rural mail delivery, a telegram! With trembling fingers Daddy ripped it open. "Dear Mom and Dad, I am fine. Be home soon. Love, Hershel." A world renewed! Reborn!

Joy and squeals of wonder. He was alive! He was well! He was coming home!

Much later he would tell us about that long journey home: A trip filled with sorrow as he recalled what had happened. His dear friend, the chaplain would never come home to his lovely wife. His children would never know the courageous man trying to help his men, the terrified wounded young sailors, when the ship went down.

Hershel did not want to talk; those around him wished to befriend him, but he remained silent. The memories continued, for he could not turn his mind from the tragedy. His young friends who worked on the flight deck with him were dead. He thought of their families and knew their grief would never cease. He wondered why his life had been spared. His ship had been hit by two Kamikaze planes and had sunk almost immediately off the coast of Iwo Jima.

He slept fitfully and over and over recalled the agony of the sinking ship. In his nightmares he relived the actual happenings. He was again in the water, trying to keep afloat, while the Japanese planes continued strafing, trying to kill those who had escaped from the doomed aircraft carrier. The four hours in the water seemed an eternity. At last a ship arrived to rescue those who remained alive.

He came home on the bus from the nearest town, getting off at the end of the country dirt road. The whole neighborhood watched and waited for him, ever since the telegram had arrived. Noah and Lee Cooper saw him first and they joined him in his walk. At the next house Veva and Thurman Robinson walked along with the group. They told us about the conversation. "Are you sure you are all right?" they asked. "Yes, I'm fine, except I have trouble sleeping. My friends on the flight deck, most all were killed."

"What happened to your ship?"

"We suffered two direct hits. No time to prepare. My friend, the chaplain, the last time I saw him he was trying to help the injured sailors. He didn't make it."

Noah put a hand out to touch the sailor's arm, "I'm sorry, Hersh, I'm so terribly sorry."

"Why him and not me? Oh, God, war is so horrible! I keep dreaming of the sinking ship and the suicide planes."

When Aunt Altie and Uncle Will saw him, they came running out to the road.

"Oh, thank the Lord, you're safe!" Aunt Altie hugged him fiercely to her ample bosom while tears slid slowly down her wrinkled cheeks. The sailor was silent. He had said all he could bear to say. They walked along quietly.

They passed the big tree that grew near the center of the road in front of Uncle Joe's house, passed the graveyard where his grandparents and relatives were buried, and then as they topped the small knoll he could see the farm house. "It's just like I imagined it a million times since I left!" He hurried now. He was almost home.

Home at last! A safe place from the tragedies of war! No stopping to knock on the door. He came through the center hallway and called their names, "Mom, Dad, anybody home?"

"He's home! He's home!" I left the dishes I had been washing in the kitchen and ran. Mama hugged him tightly, arms flung around his shoulders while tears flowed down her face as she shook with emotion. Weeping with joy, we all tried to touch him as we wiped tears away with the backs of our hands.

Hessie and Albert Spier heard the commotion from across the road where they lived and came running. They each hugged him tightly, and Hessie, who weighed almost 300 pounds, started pounding Hershel's back, and with each blow (which I thought would surely knock him out) kept exclaiming, "We are so glad, so glad, so glad, you are home safely!"

Daddy, the strong farmer who seldom showed any emotion, cried openly, while saying with amazement, as if to reassure himself, "He came home, he really came home!"

Epilogue

Hershel was given a month-long survival furlough and then sent back to Saipan. Thankfully, by that time, the war was winding down. He was mustered out of the Navy in May of 1946. He came back to Arkansas to live where he married a local girl, Reba Chism, and they had one child, Carolyn.

On February 21, 1945, the USS Bismarck Sea was the last US Navy aircraft carrier to be lost to enemy action during World War II. 605 officers and men of the 923 crew members were rescued, many picked up by destroyer escorts, the same type of ship that my husband served on during World War II.

Captain of the ship, John L. Pratt, gave an excellent first-person account of the sinking of the USS Bismarck Sea. It includes the heroic actions of several individuals, including Chaplain Shannon, who was Hershel's friend.

UNDYING HOPE

D addy was one of many cotton farmers who worked long hours with little reward for his efforts. Many borrowed money to buy seed to plant their crops each spring. Daddy was not one of them. He always paid with cash.

Disaster loomed when the weather failed to cooperate. Because of the possibility of flood or drought, seed was sown generously, hoping a "good stand of cotton" might survive. Crop insurance was unheard of during my growing-up years.

Daddy watched anxiously as rain, descending in torrents, washed the precious seed away, or left seed to rot in the ground before it could sprout. Farmers replanted after extensive damage, sometimes more than once. In low-lying areas only a portion of the field might require redoing.

We looked closely for new growth to emerge in the furrows. After the young plants were well established, a tedious operation called "choppin' cotton" began. We thinned the plants using a hoe, and in the same process, removed the grass and weeds that choked the growth. During this period the farmer prayed for enough rain to keep his fields healthy and strong. When the clouds failed to produce rain, the sun beat relentlessly down and destroyed the crops before maturity. My father lamented, "Everything's all burned up."

Farmers faced another problem when insects invaded the fields and ruined the entire region. Poison purchased to spray the plants added to the expenses.

When we "hired out" to chop cotton, we received 50 to 75 cents for an eight-hour day. My family worked in our fields from daylight until dark, but never on a Sunday. We had an hour off for lunch. Daddy never paid his children "except for our keep." Working in the stifling hot sun, with no rest periods or cold drinks, left us exhausted.

I wanted to please my parents, and as I grew older I worked hard, seldom complaining. As a teenager I tried to tell Daddy how much work I accomplished. I doubt he ever realized his stinging rebuke, "You don't even earn your salt," caused so much pain.

Growing up while working in the cotton patch is not unique. Many farm children shared my background. My friend, Ellen, from Georgia, spoke to a church group telling them how hard she worked in the cotton field. In her soft southern drawl she said, "I was the best little 'hoer' my father had." When snickers turned into laughter, she realized her poor choice of words.

Finally the crops were "laid-by." We could do nothing further to produce a successful crop: weeding, plowing, fertilizing, or spraying. Many weeks passed before the cotton developed fully and the bolls burst open displaying the fluffy white harvest.

For the hard labor of "pickin' cotton" the going rate started at 35 to 50 cents per one hundred pounds. If the cotton did not develop properly, our fingers tore open the stunted bolls, our skin often torn by the sharp burs. Then the small amount of cotton was "hard to come by," as Daddy said.

Autumn—cotton pickin' time! We picked with both hands, as we removed cotton from individual bolls and deposited in a long sack dragged between the rows. When the sack became too heavy to pull, we struggled to hoist the bundle over one shoulder to carry to the scales for "weigh in." The sack, made of heavy duck material with a shoulder strap, opened near the waist and extended behind the worker on the ground about eight feet. The material eventually wore through on the bottom. Mama patched the holes with yardage from the store.

Cotton pickers challenged one another to make work more interesting. We often pushed ourselves to the limit. "Want to bet a quarter who'll win at picking cotton today?" Cousins Orison and Audrey competed, and kept a running account when sacks were weighed. One day, Audrey won by 5 pounds.

We spent days, sometimes weeks, picking enough cotton to fill the wagon bed with high sideboards. With the wagon filled to the top, we took another load to the cotton gin. I, along with my brother and sister, rode to the gin on top of the wagon in the loose white cotton. We sprawled on our backs, sinking into the soft mass as it covered our bare legs and arms. We gazed into the blue sky and watched fleecy white clouds floating above in various forms. In our imagination, cats, dogs, chickens, and cows drifted overhead.

Two horses pulled the wagon on the leisurely trip to the cotton gin located a few miles away. The owner, Mr. Eads, greeted us warmly and seemed to enjoy that we watched the activity.

Daddy yelled above the noise, "Watch how that large pipe sucks the cotton up and into the gin. Marvelous invention, the cotton gin. Removes all the seeds and debris."

He then took us to a room filled with fluffy white cotton. In another section, seed accumulated in large mounds.

During the final step, the cotton, compressed into a large bale, was bound with steel straps, ready to be taken to our nearby town of Morrilton, Arkansas. During the depression years, the 500 pound bale of cotton brought five to seven cents per pound, $25 to $35 a bale.

Mr. Eads charged $5.00 per bale to gin the cotton. Daddy

hauled the finished bounty home in the wagon to await taking to market. We carried the seeds home in sacks. Later we took them to the compress mill to be ground into hulls and meal, for feeding cattle.

Daddy tried to out-guess the market and sell when the price was high, or delay selling when the price dropped. Many times he misjudged, selling just before the price rose or failing to sell before a nosedive.

Our family occasionally returned to the cotton field after the main picking, to collect bits of cotton called "goose locks." I recall one year we kids completed the job. Cold dreary weather with frost had destroyed the green foliage. The leaves hung lank and withered, and the remaining pieces of white cotton stood out in contrast against a background of brown. Our fingers were pierced as we pried cotton from under-developed, stunted bolls. We wore apron-type holders made from flour sacks, tied around our waists. Only tiny bits, of "scrappin' cotton," remained in the bolls. Whatever we gathered earned a few more pennies for our family. We shivered against the biting frost, and with icy hands hurried to finish the task to escape the cold.

Daddy's life as a cotton farmer was not one of ease. The actual cash realized seldom supplied adequate shelter, food and clothing. Daddy faced life with courage, determined to succeed. Springtime brought new hopes of abundant crops and greater financial gain.

MEMORIES OF BUDDY

D addy reacted with overwhelming sorrow and remorse when he injured my four-year-old brother in an accident. I arrived home from school and Buddy met me with a huge white bandage covering the lower part of one side of his face. I was horrified. His blue eyes looked frightened.

Mama explained what happened. "Your Dad was cutting trees down in the pasture for firewood. Just as he swung the big axe for another blow at a tree trunk, Buddy ran up right behind him!" The axe cut through the skin and into Buddy's mouth, somehow missing the teeth and the jawbone.

"Look, Rita," Mama exclaimed, "You can see if he'd been a few inches closer, no telling what might have happened!"

Daddy must have been appalled at the horrible sight. Fortunately, the axe had a corner broken off or greater damage would have occurred.

My father's face was etched in agony when he returned home from work that night. Although he could not foresee Buddy running up behind him, he felt guilty. Stitches to close the wound left a scar my brother still carries. The whole family was terribly shaken by the accident.

My father acted very differently over other incidents in Buddy's childhood.

When Buddy was six years old, the iceman came to our house and told Daddy a lemon was missing from his truck. We bought lemons on special occasions for making lemonade and to serve with fish. Buddy had taken a lemon, hid it, and Daddy found it high up in the pecan tree. I've always wondered where he knew to look.

Daddy took Buddy inside the house and said, "I'll have to spank you, because you took something that did not belong to you. That's called stealing and our family does not steal."

"Please, Daddy," Buddy cried, "Don't hit me. I'll be good."

"I've got to teach you a lesson!" Daddy said, "I can see that you can't be trusted." My father thought the spanking necessary and it left red marks on the tender white skin.

At that moment I loved my baby brother more than ever before and I felt rage at my father. I thought the punishment too severe for the offense, but I knew my parents did not tolerate stealing and telling lies.

More punishment lay ahead. Daddy marched Buddy to the tree where he hid the lemon. He unfastened a trace chain from the horses' harness and placed the chain around Buddy's tiny waist, he then locked my little brother to the tree. Child abuse was a term never heard then and Daddy did not consider his actions to be either immoral or illegal.

"There," he said, "You'll have plenty of time to think about what you did." He left Buddy chained to the tree during the long, hot afternoon. Mama brought her little son several glasses of cold water before the day was over. She did not agree with the cruel punishment, but she did not interfere.

My dad talked a lot about the incident over the years, as if he felt vindicated for the punishment he meted out for his youngest son.

Daddy had a blacksmith anvil in the workshop where he repaired and made parts for farm equipment. The anvil, constructed of heavy forged iron, was shaped with a point that allowed Dad to work on small pieces.

The two young Spier boys played with Buddy almost every day. When my brother was seven, the three decided to cut off the pointed end of the anvil. They took turns sawing with Dad's hacksaw. The mischief continued without anyone discovering what they were doing.

Daddy was angry. "Must have taken those little peckerwoods several weeks to do that! I can't believe that we didn't find them in time to make them stop!" By the time the boys were grown, Daddy thought the story was funny.

I have no idea if Daddy spanked Buddy or informed the neighbors what their kids did. For even minor offenses, the leather belt inflicted a few licks across our legs or bottom.

One summer the young boys swiped Mama's iron teakettle, breaking the antique into dozens of irregular-shaped pieces to shoot in their bean-flips. Bean-flips were made with a y-shaped piece of wood. Rubber strips cut from inner tubes were attached to the wood and to a piece of leather from an old shoe tongue. The leather served as a pouch for the projectile. Every farm boy carried a bean-flip.

The "shots" made of cast-iron could be deadly missiles for rabbits, squirrels, rats, and birds. My parents warned my brother not to kill song birds. They did allow the shooting of sparrows that occupied the barn rafters and carried lice. Stones and pebbles picked up from the ground usually served as ammunition. Fortunately, no serious injuries ever occurred.

Not many details were available to me about Buddy's growing up years. He was only seven when I left the farm. I seldom received a letter from home. Mama was the only person who wrote and many details were sketchy. The farmhouse had no phone. Even if we owned one, long distance telephone expenses were considered too costly. I depended on Uncle Roy and Aunt Nora to take me whenever they planned a trip to see the country relatives. Those visits were several months apart.

During my early years of working in Little Rock, and later when I was working in California, I bought gifts for my entire family for Christmas. I made a special effort to buy presents for Buddy, usually inexpensive gifts for I had little money to spend. I bought color books and crayons, a bat and ball, a basketball, a catcher's mitt, and finally, a Daisy air rifle, his beloved BB gun. "I will never forget your sending me the gifts!" Buddy told me. "I loved the BB gun more than you will ever know!"

Once while visiting Arkansas from California I asked Buddy to come and sit on my lap. He said, "Awe, Sis, don't you think I am getting a little too big for that?" And he truly was, for he had grown tall and gangly.

I caught up on family events during summer visits. My husband Bill snapped pictures of farm scenes of Lewis and our family throughout the years. I missed the big occasions in my brother's life: his decision to accept Christ and be baptized, high school graduation, his first car, the first date.

After Buddy was grown he lived for a short time with Cousins Clarence and Mae Ruth in Dinuba, California when Bill and I stopped to visit. The phone rang. When I answered it, a young man asked to speak to Lewis (Buddy's real name). I said, "He's not here right now, but this is Lewis' big sister." The caller laughed and said, "I don't know you, but I know Lewis. If you are bigger than he is, you are some woman!" Buddy, my baby brother, had gotten to be six feet 2 inches.

When Bill and I lived in the first house we purchased in Monterey Park, California, Lewis came to visit. Somewhere there is a picture of us together, with my baby brother towering over me.

We were delighted when he married, Gay. We rejoiced when

their first child, Tawnia was born. Three years later his wife gave birth to another baby, Crystal. Lewis felt great joy over the new child, but was devastated when complications threatened his wife's life. He called me by phone, pouring out his despair. I tried to comfort him.

When his wife recovered fully and their little daughter came home healthy, we praised God for answered prayer.

Many years later Lewis baby-sat his little granddaughter, Kacie, when she suffered from colic. He lulled her to sleep by running the vacuum sweeper and walking until she fell asleep in his arms.

While on a visit to the farm, he held my small granddaughter Shayda in his arms, asking, "How's my little darlin' today?"

After Lewis and Gay married, they welcomed us when we visited them in Arkansas. Their generosity extended to "make yourselves at home" and involved using the washing machine and dryer. One day I decided to do the laundry quickly, using as little water from their well as possible. I tossed all of my clothes together in one big load. And I got caught!

Gay said, "Loretta Mehl, what do you think you're doing?" When she told Lewis, he came to the wash place to check on me. Laughing as he put his arm around my shoulders he said, "Honey, don't you know that light and dark clothes should be kept separate? Didn't anyone ever teach you how to do the washin' yet?"

I always knew I was loved by Lewis.

I Leave Home

⬥⬥◆⬥⬥

Daddy and Mama never talked to me about my leaving home. I made no definite plans regarding my future, but one thing I vowed repeatedly, "I'm going to escape the farm as soon as I graduate from high school."

The love for the family farm that sustained my father, failed to excite me. Blinded by self-pity, I overlooked the beauty in the rising sun falling across meadows where cattle grazed peacefully. To me, fresh vegetables from the garden represented sweat-drenched toil during hours of planting, weeding, and picking produce. I disliked the hard, backbreaking work of chopping cotton and corn and detested milking cows, slopping pigs, and feeding baby calves.

I despised my life of painful, embarrassing poverty. I retained vivid memories of socks with threadbare heels, inexpensive oxford shoes with battered toes and paper-thin soles and dresses sewn from cheap cotton material. I felt ashamed of our house and second-hand furniture bought when my parents married and never replaced.

Without electricity, we lacked electric lights, refrigerator, vacuum cleaner or other appliances. Telephone lines were not installed in our area.

High in iron and minerals, our water, drawn from a deep well, smelled and tasted like rotten eggs. It stained everything it touched: clothing, dishes, and cooking utensils. Mama cooked on a wood-burning stove that also heated water for cleaning and bathing. In the outdoor privy behind our house we used an old catalog for toilet paper. Bathing consisted of a hurried wipe-down with a torn rag or soaking in a galvanized wash tub.

The coming graduation day motivated me to excel in school. Education seemed my way out of poverty. As commencement approached, Mama purchased yardage for my dress. Aunt Tennie copied the pattern from the Sears Catalog, and measured me before cutting the material. She then stitched the pieces together to complete my wardrobe for the big event. I borrowed stockings from Cousin Mae Ruth and white shoes from my cousin's wife, Veva.

Daddy and Mama did not attend my graduation; I rode with other graduates and their relatives on the school bus. Daddy refused to discuss the occasion, so Mama stayed home with him. Perhaps he felt insecure in an unfamiliar setting. Maybe it hurt too much to see me receive a high school diploma when he had no "book learnin'." Whatever his reason, he made my accomplishment seem unimportant, even though I was first to earn a high school diploma in our immediate family.

Sunday, after my graduation, Aunt Nora and Uncle Roy from Little Rock came to visit. I asked if I could go home with them and look for a job.

"Of course you can," they said. My parents kept their children from time to time during the summer months.

My total wealth consisted of ten dollars my family gave me for graduation. I carried my possessions in a large paper sack. I wore my one good dress and my only pair of shoes.

My mother wiped away tears and my father's face looked strained as I hugged them, kissed my little brother goodbye, and hurried out to Uncle Roy's car. I was seventeen years old and inexperienced for job hunting and living in the city.

My parents did not beg me to stay; I think they wished for peace in the household. I constantly complained and taunted them that I planned to leave.

Located just down the road, we stopped at Aunt Altie's house. "Goodbye, honey," she sighed, as she wrapped me in her arms. "Good luck at finding a job in the city. We will miss you." With those words, tears flooded my eyes and I felt overwhelmed by sadness and loss. The fearful unknown stretched before me.

Newspaper ads listed many jobs. War industries competed with Western Union Telegraph Company for easy-to-train employees. I applied for work as telegraph operator, passed the tests and started training immediately. Company rules forbade my sending and receiving telegrams on the wire until my eighteenth birthday.

I found living in the city strange and alarming. I did not grasp how to catch a bus for different locations or how the streets and house numbers ran. Neither did I know how to operate modern conveniences and appliances. To provide another change of clothing, Aunt Nora bought me a blouse and cotton skirt.

A short time after I moved in with my relatives, Uncle Roy's company transferred him. Forced to find a place to live, I chose an inexpensive boarding house where a lady advertised for a roommate to share the rent.

America still waged World War II, and soldiers from nearby Camp Robinson flooded the city of Little Rock. Servicemen standing on every corner whistled at me. Once after working the 11:00 PM shift, a soldier marched the entire way home alongside of me, with one hand tucked inside his jacket as if he held a gun. I was too naive to be afraid. Another time a young sailor tried to initiate a conversation. I ignored him and headed for my work office. He followed and called my name. I turned to recognize Howard, cousin Mary Dale's husband. I could safely talk to him, a relief.

I maintained strict rules about attending Sunday school, church, and BYPU (Baptist Young Peoples Union) meetings. At church I met young soldiers; many were lonesome and looking for someone to listen and talk to them. My girlfriends dated some of them, and eventually, I did too. My friends introduced me to a young man from Indiana. Gene and I dined at inexpensive restaurants, attended church activities, and walked to the service club, where we took our Bibles and read Scriptures together. We clasped hands and after several dates, he kissed me and then left, whistling softly into the night.

Gene pleaded that I remain in Little Rock, but when Western Union transferred me upon my request, to the Los Angeles office, I was happy to go. He asked to visit me after the war, but I did not encourage him and he did not write again.

Soon after I arrived in California, I attended the First Baptist Church of Alhambra. One Sunday I lingered by the side entrance to the sanctuary, listening to the choir rehearse my favorite hymn, *Amazing Grace.* The song reminded me of home and I felt lonely for familiar faces and hugs. Stan, a member of my Sunday school class, strolled to my side with a tall, blonde young man, "I want you to meet Bill Mehl, who's also new in our church."

I was intrigued. Bill smiled at me with a crooked smile and stood tall with military bearing. He had just returned home from the Navy. He was older than I, and more sophisticated than the boys in Arkansas. Our backgrounds were dissimilar. He seemed fascinated by my southern drawl, "Say something, anything," he teased. I thought it a sure sign he liked me.

On our first date, he took me to a football game at the Rose Bowl. I knew nothing about football. He taught me. We attended movies, beach parties and church activities. I was thrilled to be escorted to the Hollywood Bowl, Pasadena Playhouse, and the

Huntington Library. We drove to the mountains and the nearby beaches.

We dated only a few months before Bill asked me to marry him. I was not ready and waited for two years before I said "yes." We married on September 11, 1948.

Our traditional wedding invitations read: "Mr. and Mrs. Arthur Miller invite you to attend the wedding of their daughter, Loretta." I knew my parents would not attend, nor did they share the expenses. For our simple wedding I selected a full skirted gown of white satin with sweetheart neckline and fitted bodice. I found my dress on the sale rack, marked below cost.

I chose my sister, who had recently moved to nearby Lancaster, California, as my only attendant. A friend lent me a dress for Opal to wear. A note arrived the day before the wedding stating that she, her husband, and baby son were going to the county fair instead.

My eyes were red from weeping, as I practiced my vows at the wedding rehearsal.

Marian, a new friend from Sunday school, who later married Stan, agreed to be my maid of honor. She borrowed a full-length pink gown and carried the lavender bouquet I ordered for my sister. Few people guessed that she was a last minute replacement.

Bill and I chose the Pasadena Chapel of Roses, a well-known site decorated with fresh flowers and tall candles, a bride's room for dressing and picture taking, and a staircase to toss my bouquet of white carnations. We paid $40.00 for the use of the chapel. Our minister, Rev. Leslie Eads, performed the ceremony. Cousin Bob Spier, my only family member in attendance, walked me down the aisle.

At our fiftieth anniversary celebration, Bob announced, "When I give the bride away, she stays in the marriage!"

Many years later Bill still declared, "I can show you the exact spot where we met!"

PLENTY TO LAST

L iving in our sharecropper's shack, and even later at the farmhouse we purchased, money was always in short supply. We seldom bought anything we could do without. We used whatever items were available.

One of these articles was a ready supply of cloth that came to the farm in the form of sacks used to hold flour, cornmeal, sugar, and feed for the livestock. The unbleached yardage bore the printed information giving the net weight, the company name, address, and advertising slogans. We first used cold water to soak the material and then worked with home-made lye soap to remove the lettering. The largest words were name brands: Buckeye Pure Gold Cornmeal, Arbuckle's Pure Cane Sugar, Red Robin Flour, and Bob White Flour (with the corresponding pictures of the birds), along with other facts.

The sacks, sewn together with heavy twine, unraveled when the proper thread was pulled. We saved the twine, winding it into large balls and used it to tie packages, to crochet around the edges of dresser scarves, and to make doilies. Mama also improvised a ball by enclosing twine in the end of an old sock and sewing it with a multitude of tiny stitches. As children we played softball and dodge ball using the home-made toy.

The sacks provided material for tablecloths, curtains, quilt linings, sheets, pillowcases, aprons, and diapers. We continually found new ways to use the material from the sacks, fashioning wearing apparel such as baby dresses, gowns, blouses, petticoats and bloomers. When the yardage was too short, Mama added a border of contrasting material to extend the length. She added embroidery to pillowcases and dresser scarves, using the briar stitch and hem stitch to add tiny embroidered roses on blouses and dresses.

I did not appreciate our boundless supply of material. Over and over as I dried dishes with sackcloth, I said that someday I would own real store-bought tea towels, which would represent the greatest luxury. I daydreamed of buying pretty clothing and felt I would be wealthy when I could purchase a non-essential like ready-made dishtowels.

The year Bill and I married we drove to Pennsylvania to visit his relatives, none of whom had ever lived on a farm. Their houses were lovely, with nice furniture, rugs, china, and silver. I felt a surge of envy.

As we ate dinner the day of our arrival, Auntie Frances said, "I've been saving something to give you." My imagination soared. Was she offering me a piece of the family silver, one of the Limoges serving plates, or a heavy linen table cloth with matching napkins? I could hardly finish eating, wondering what the gift would be.

Going to the hall closet, Auntie Frances removed a bundle tied with string. As she handed the object to me, she told me about one of the family traditions.

Her father, my husband's grandfather, had owned a grocery store. Over many years the family accumulated a huge supply of cloth sacks. Many of the commodities delivered in them were emptied into various bins and canisters. My husband's family came from thrifty, German stock, a characteristic revealed in saving the empty sacks to later divide among the members of the family.

As Auntie Frances explained what she was giving me, I looked at the bundle with astonishment. Amidst all the luxury items displayed in their house, the Mehl family treasured the sacks. I hoped my expression did not betray my true feelings. My southern heritage decreed I react with gratitude.

"Thank you," I mumbled.

"If these are not enough for you," Auntie Frances continued, "we have many more. I'd like to give you plenty to last all your married life. They make lovely tea towels."

"I'm sure these will be sufficient," I said. *Many more than enough*, I thought.

My childhood habits of thrift forbade my tossing the sacks away. During the early years of my marriage I seldom used them. Instead I bought colorful dishtowels.

As the years went by, I occasionally removed a few from the neat stack that I kept on a high shelf. From my early experience I knew that with use the material became soft and absorbent.

Eventually, I learned to appreciate the sacks. I even read an article glorifying them made into aprons and jumpers, bold printed wording across the front of the specialty clothing.

COME AND SEE

During my years of growing up I longed for a house with everything new and modern. When word reached me in California that my folks planned to build a new house, I rejoiced. The stately looking old house, painted white with dormer windows, had been home to my mother's family when they owned the farm. My father decided that the old dwelling should be demolished to build on the same location. Mama's letters failed to describe the house they were planning. I imagined that the new building would be built of brick or rock with modern appliances.

The year after Bill and I married, we made a trip to visit relatives in Arkansas. My new husband had no idea what to expect since his childhood had been so different from mine. When we drove into the driveway and parked in front of the "new" house, I faced a big disappointment. Fake brick siding covered the exterior of the frame house. There was little time for closer examination before people spilled out of the doorway to greet us with hugs and kisses. Aunt Altie and Uncle Will watched from their house across the road, "I don't know who the man is, but they are kissing him too."

Bill did not know what to make of the affectionate greetings given him as a stranger. Later that same summer, Bill's Auntie Frances addressed me quite differently in Pennsylvania when she extended a formal handshake. As Bill's new wife I expected at least a hug from family members.

Come and See

My mother, father, and brother Lewis reached out to welcome us, and Aunt Altie, Uncle Will, my brother Hershel and his wife Reba soon joined the other greeters. Everyone laughed and talked at once.

Daddy interrupted our greeting to tell me, "Come with me, I want you to see the new house." As I followed him through the living room and into the kitchen I noted new kitchen cabinets were installed. From there we inspected the three bedrooms, and one bath. Daddy appeared delighted with the new structure, but I felt my disappointment growing as we went from room to room. The inside of the house was even worse than the outside. Old lumber had been used from the original house in the construction. The doors and windows were recycled from the original building, and rough, unfinished boards framed doors, windows, and closets. None of the joints and corners fit squarely.

The floors, sometimes bare, were also made of used lumber; while cheap linoleum and inexpensive rugs covered other areas. One coat of inferior quality paint applied on the walls failed to cover completely. Different shades of pastel color used in each room nullified any coordinating efforts.

Many of the furnishings in the house were items I remembered from childhood, worn and damaged by the many years of use. Appliances and a few other items had been given to my parents by children who were ready to discard the pieces.

A lump the size of a baseball rose in my throat and the held-back tears threatened to choke me.

The iron bedstead in my parents' bedroom had been purchased when they started keeping house. A battered dresser with a long mirror was the only other piece of furniture in their bedroom

I had dreamed and yearned for a nice house for my parents all my life. Now for me, the terrible fact emerged that my desire would never be fulfilled. I knew in my heart that Daddy would never build another house.

I should have known better than to expect a nice house. Daddy and I could not understand each other. That was the crux of the matter, which always stood between us. I would never be like him and it was painful for us both. Though I had been born of his flesh and blood, our values, concerns, and life styles were vastly different. While I longed for better things in life, Daddy was satisfied to keep things the way they were.

The Gift Giving

Mama looked forward to our visits in the summertime, and she always insisted we carry gifts home from the farm to California. Once she gave us tomatoes, bell peppers, and cucumbers. A produce inspection was required when we entered near the California state border, but since we were pulling a RV, we decided to take a chance that the vegetables would be allowed through.

When stopped at the Agricultural Inspection Station, we answered truthfully that we carried vegetables from Arkansas. The officer said, "I need to check whatever you have." He examined the produce and asked, "Are you sure these were home-grown?" When I assured him they were, he declared, "Mighty fine looking vegetables. I must take this one pepper with a small hole."

Mama harvested pecans that grew in the back yard from a tree planted by her mother decades before. She cracked the nuts on a chopping block with a hammer she stored in the wash place. She picked up pecans every fall, not just for her own use, but for the joy of sharing.

Once when she offered pecans, I said, "Mama, why don't you keep them to make pies?" Her brown eyes looked sad as she replied, "Then I wouldn't have anything to give you!" I could not refuse her gift of love.

I deeply regret a hard lesson I learned from an earlier occasion about accepting gifts. The occasion happened when our first child,

Charles Arthur, was born. We were so happy to have a son and named him for his two grandfathers, since he was born on his grandfather Charles' 62nd birthday.

Mama sent a baby dress embroidered with flowers in bright, multi-colored thread, I thought the dress too fancy for a baby boy so I returned it. Sending the dress back seemed the natural thing to do, for our family always donated items we could not use. I did not realize my response might be misunderstood.

I sent a note explaining why I was returning the gift. "Thank you for the baby dress. I am returning it, for boy babies no longer wear dresses where we live. Perhaps you could present it to someone there who needs it. Thank you for thinking of us."

Twenty-three years old, I was immature at assessing another person's feelings. The dress did not seem practical or useful. A young mother in the office where I worked gave me a plentiful supply of clothing that her small son had outgrown.

We lived on a GI allotment check of $85.00 per month. Money for diapers, or baby equipment, would have eased our financial squeeze. We bought used baby furniture that Bill repaired and repainted. I realized the lack of money was our problem, and I learned years earlier not to expect any help from my parents.

Mama did not "tell me off," but my sister blasted me at the first opportunity during my next visit home. The greeting was not what I expected or wanted to hear. She "raked me over the coals real good" and said how insensitive I'd acted. I do not recall everything she said, but one thing I clearly remember: "Better to burn the dress, than hurt Mama by returning it." My sibling's hostile reaction made me wonder if she had sewn the dress or perhaps bought it at a yard sale. My mother never confronted me about the event. She never, ever, mentioned what her thoughts had been.

I learned from that experience not to refuse gifts, even though traveling home with some items proved difficult. After leaving the farm, I once accidentally left the pecan halves in Pennsylvania, and Cousin Mary gave them to a lady who baked pecan pies for a church social. Another time I forgot the pecans in my son Charlie's refrigerator, and he and his family ate the nuts with their cereal. I never told Mama. She would have been hurt to know that I had forgotten her gifts. I never intentionally caused pain for Mama or Daddy.

In the late 1950s, while home on vacation, Daddy surprised me with a gift. He cut down cedar trees on the farm and planed the lumber to construct a cedar chest. Uncle John built the chest and Daddy presented his gift when I arrived. We had a big problem in transporting the large box home. Bill covered it with a tarp and lashed it onto the top of our car. Our gift looked exactly like a coffin. We received many strange glances as we traveled across country to our home in California.

Several years before Daddy died he distributed substantial money to his four children. I was shocked. He explained, "I don't want the government to have my money." He referred to inheritance taxes and costs of settling his estate. I wanted to be happy about his generous gift, but instead wished my parents had spent the money to make their lives better. I had to conceal my emotions and thank my parents for their generosity. The money meant little to me, for most of my family's financial hardships were over. By that time, Bill and I owned a beautiful house, swimming pool, cars, and an RV.

After my parents' died and the trust account was divided, I felt much the same way. I couldn't stop thinking about the sacrifices and the hard life that produced my inheritance. I told Bill that when I consider all the things Mama and Daddy could have enjoyed with their money, I only want to cry.

I know Daddy wished to leave something for the kids, for that is what he told my son, David when he visited the farm. None of us really needed the money, for we had made it on our own. As a down payment on our first house, I borrowed $1,500 from Daddy in 1951, at the going rate of 3% interest. We repaid the debt quickly.

I wanted to rejoice and be glad about the gifts of money and the inheritance. I talked about it with my husband. Instead I could not help thinking how Mama and Daddy bought cheap goods, skimped, and saved for 71 years. I begged them to come to California for a visit. Daddy never came and Mama only one time. I never had one telephone call from them and received few cards for special occasions. They sent me a Bible before my marriage, and one summer after I married, Daddy drove me to town and bought me a dress.

At Christmastime for several years, Daddy sent each child in my family a dollar bill. When the kids were older, he sent the family ten dollars. I put a dollar on the tree for the children from their grandparents, and spent the rest to buy a turkey for our holiday dinner.

I'm not ungrateful to my parents for the money. I'm glad that our financial situation enables us to give generously to our offspring. I realize my parents' legacy may provide financial benefits that will reach not only me, but my children and future generations. We have contributed down payments on houses, music lessons for our talented grandkids, and helped pay for flutes, violins, and saxophone. We donated money to Scout conferences, church camping trips, singing tours, and other special requests.

I wanted nice things for my parents more than they did, especially Daddy. However, I think Mama would have enjoyed a nice house, furnishings, clothing, and the small joys of being able to buy items that would have enriched her spirit. Near the end of

Mama's life, one of the caregivers told me about helping Jewell count her money in her pocketbook. She had $1.27. That amount seemed symbolic. To me it represented the poverty of how Mama had lived, even with thousands of dollars in invested holdings. The money carried her name, but did not truly belong to her. Daddy controlled it while he was alive, and then my sister allocated the spending money for Mama's care until her death in 1998.

THE DIVIDING FENCE

T he rusted, barbed wire fence with the irregular weather-stained posts symbolized a relationship, which had united, but eventually separated, the two families. The fence, intertwined with honeysuckle vines, poison ivy and persimmon bushes, stood as the common boundary line that divided the Miller and Scoggins farms.

Members of both families lived in the Hill Creek community long before the building of the fence. The farms belonged to earlier generations before the properties were transferred to relatives, the present owners. The relationship between the two families grew much like the tangled vines and bushes in the old fence row. Events jumbled together in no set pattern, interspersed with major happenings.

My mother, Jewell, and her friend, Ethel, had been school classmates and went to singing school together. They often talked for a few minutes as their paths crossed, coming or going to their separate farmhouses. The neighbors visited back and forth almost every weekend. The women helped one another when they had a quilt ready to finish quilting.

Likewise, my father Arthur, and Ethel's husband, Orville, worked together when hog killing time rolled around or an extra hand was needed when harvesting corn, cotton, or alfalfa. They shared rides as they went "off to town" to buy groceries or equipment. The neighbors rejoiced together when children were born and grieved when family members or friends were laid to rest in the little country cemetery.

Although the personalities were dissimilar, no conscious effort was made to conform a person to another's viewpoint. Peculiar character traits or flaws were accepted. Even though they thought differently about many things, neighbors were people who needed one another.

The two women exchanged surplus food as easily as they exchanged their favorite recipes or quilt block patterns. Ethel brought a mess of turnip greens when she came to visit. The friends quilted while we children played marbles or jacks. When Ethel started to leave, Jewell was apt to say, "You wait a minute while I get a poke sack and we'll gather some okra for your dinner tonight. It's growin' so fast I can't keep up with it." Sacks of beans, cucumbers, tomatoes, or whatever was plentiful found its way home with the neighbor.

We kids played underfoot while we listened to bits of conversation.

"Well, Jewell," Ethel said, "Our kids are growin' so fast, someday they'll all be grown and there'll be just two old women sittin' by the fireside and gossipin'." They laughed together. Neither expressed concern that the time might arrive very fast. Their lives were filled with work and they lamented that days never seemed long enough for planting, weeding, harvesting, and countless other chores on the farm.

"Been cannin' up some sauerkraut," Ethel said one day. "Left that stuff sittin' out by the well shed and it got so sour almost blew the top off the crock!"

"Oh, my goodness sakes," Jewell shook her head, "Must've been sittin' too long in the hot sun. Good thing you found it before waitin' any longer. Wouldn't want all that work to go to waste."

At last the children grew up and Jewell and Ethel found themselves alone much of the time—the prediction came true, and they became even closer friends. The children married and moved away with the exception of the Miller's youngest son, my brother Lewis. He married a local girl and asked permission to buy the family farm. Our parents, happy to grant his request, wanted an heir to enjoy the benefits of working the land they loved.

I took a far-different path, but returned for vacations almost every year. Mama, Daddy, and my siblings and their families shared what happened while I was away.

Lewis, a progressive farmer, bought modern equipment and studied improved farm methods. He built a mechanized dairy barn and installed automatic milking and cooling systems while increasing the size of the dairy herd.

When I returned one summer Lewis told me about the quarrel between he and the Scoggins. I pressed him for details and my brother's voice revealed the depths of his sorrow and frustration as he related what had happened, many times using the exact words as he remembered them.

He said he was driving around the farm one day and noticed the old fence row, the posts standing askew and the wire hanging loose and almost rusted through. He knew that Mr. Orville rented out the adjoining pastureland. The cattle grazing there looked unhealthy, some had pinkeye. The disease could spread to his herd if the fence broke down. He'd considered replacing the fence before, but now it seemed urgent. He mentioned it to Daddy who said he thought it was a good idea, but that he hoped Mr. Orville would be willing to share the cost.

However, Lewis said he was the one concerned about the fence and he would not ask the neighbors to pay.

Lewis drove over to see Mr. Orville and Ms. Ethel. "I've been over on the hill lookin' at that old fence that runs between our farms. It's in pretty bad shape, wire's all rusted through and posts rotted out at the ground. The whole thing needs replacing. If it's all right with you, I'll clean up that old fence row and put a new fence back on the boundary line."

Orville said, "Sounds okay with me if you're willing to do all the work and pay for the fence." Ethel agreed.

Lewis started the project immediately. The undergrowth of vines and brush were removed first and the fence taken down. Lewis and the hired hand ran the fence line from corner-to-corner from where the old posts still stood. Then using a guide, they dug the postholes for the new posts, and strung the new wire for the fence.

"Sure looks better," he told our parents. "It was a big job and I'm glad to have it finally finished.

Several weeks later he heard the shocking news that Orville and Ethel spread a rumor the fence encroached on their land and was not replaced on the original property line. Lewis realized his neighbors had filed a lawsuit when he received a summons to appear in court.

"I couldn't believe it," Lewis said. "We've been friends for as long as I could remember! I had to hire a lawyer!"

"Hard to believe what happened," my father said. "After all you've done—all that work and not even asking them for one cent!"

My mother shook with anger. "Why would they think Lewis tried to cheat them out of any land? We've never done nothin' like that in our entire lives!"

"Dadgumit if I know," Lewis replied. "I knew the fence stood exactly on the line. We measured it, and it was right."

Whenever the two families met in church and community

gatherings, they reacted with sullen silence. Mama said she missed the friendly relationship the two women enjoyed. Arthur and Orville no longer helped one another with the farm work or shared rides into town for shopping. No hands lifted in greeting as their trucks passed and no one stopped for short visits.

Lewis had grown up with the Scoggin's children, and the parents could always be depended upon for help when needed. Arthur and Jewell agonized over the broken relationship as the summer days dragged by and loneliness and suspicion continued between the two families.

"What a ridiculous thing to cause so much hard feelings," Lewis told his wife, Gay. "Wish to heaven none of this had ever happened."

"You didn't do a single thing to cause a fallin' out," Gay tried to console him, "Don't go blaming yourself."

When the case was filed at the county court house it caught the attention of Mr. Edgar Gordon, a cousin of the Scoggins', who worked there. He drove out to the farm to look at the situation. He checked the corner posts and found the fence perfectly aligned. He informed his cousins their lawsuit was ill founded. The Scoggins checked the county court house records of aerial photos, but were not convinced until Mr. Gordon "pulled the chain" (the official measurement), showing the fence correct.

Jewell and Arthur suffered along with their son throughout the ordeal. For friends to bring a lawsuit against their son was, in their eyes, an unforgivable offense, and unless the Scoggins made the first move for reconciliation, there would be no mending of the relationship. The whole community knew what happened, and that made the situation worse. Everyone felt badly, but no one knew what to do about it.

The old, broken-down barbed wire fence had long since been

replaced, but there would be no putting back to normal the way things were before the quarrel erupted between the two families over the boundary line.

Epilogue

That episode ended the life-long relationship between the older members of the two families. No one wished to apologize. Each felt his reputation damaged. The Scoggins family changed churches and a new road made it possible to go the other direction to make the trip to town.

The years flew by. Ethel, Orville, Jewell and Arthur, grew old and infirm, but the quarrel was never mended.

Their children spoke when they happened to meet, which was seldom, since most lived elsewhere. Once when I visited the farm, I called Ethel. She seemed delighted to hear from me and said, "I always loved your mother." I begged Ethel to go see her, but she never did, and I did not tell Mama I made that call.

Orville died first. My parents did not attend the funeral, an unheard of thing in the rural community when I grew up. People told me my father was severely criticized for not being there.

The members of the older generation are all gone now. I feel a deep sadness that some kind of forgiveness was never exchanged. The neighbor-helping-neighbor friendship was lost the day a lawsuit was filed regarding the boundary line.

After his father died, Tim, the grandson of Mr. Orville, inherited the farm. Tim attended both Daddy's and Mama's funerals and he and my brother, Lewis, are good neighbors and friends. The two have never discussed the matter that caused all the hard feelings.

STANDING FIRM

T wo huge oak trees stand in the front yard at the farm where five generations of my family have lived. Mama said, "Those trees have been growing there for as long as I can remember." She played underneath the shade as a little girl when she lived in the original house. When I was a child, the trees provided a landmark for people coming along the road and looking for the A.D. Miller home. The driveway, which was never paved, ran along one side of the trees, continued alongside the house and all the way to the barn. The dirt, although hard-packed from use, sent up clouds of dust in the hot, dry summer.

Located close to the road, the trees gave welcome shade for parking cars when friends visited. I suppose, although I've never asked, people once parked buggies, wagons and horses there, too.

A large steel cable hanging from one of the trees provided a swing for the children. Once it held an old discarded tire, but more often the swing was made with a tow sack filled with corn husks or old rags and tied to the cable.

As children, we drew it back as far as possible, and taking a running leap, swung high in the air. Usually there were other kids there and the one on the swing begged, "Push me! High as you can! Higher, higher, push me higher." As the momentum decreased, the swing came to a standstill. Often a youngster would decide to turn around and around in a short circle, twisting the cable, winding it tightly. Their feet lifted from the ground, leaving the child to unwind, going faster and faster in a dizzy spin. The swing furnished a constant source of enjoyment and children were entertained for hours, sitting there and floating through the air.

We were amazed the stately oaks remained intact despite thunder and lightning storms and occasional tornadoes. Limbs were sometimes blown off and lightning struck other trees in the area, but the beautiful oaks remained practically untouched. As the years sped by we sometimes found dead wood caught in the upper branches and we avoided playing underneath. My parents advised against parking cars underneath during high winds or stormy weather.

Many years after I left home, people in our community were thrilled when electricity came to our valley. Then several years later, the farmers were told that the road needed to be widened and the electric company planned to install new poles and lines to accommodate the project. Arrangements to install the electric lines were discussed, for our oak trees were in the pathway.

The foreman came to tell my elderly father. "Mr. Miller," he said, "We're going to have to cut some big limbs off your oak trees."

"Well," Daddy replied slowly, "I don't think so. Don't want no one cuttin' on my trees."

"I don't think you understand, Mr. Miller," the man said. "It's necessary in order to run the electric line where we need to install it."

"Guess we will just have to see about that!" Daddy said, ending the conversation.

Several years later my grown son, David, visited the farm and noticed something very strange about the electric line. It ran along our side of the farm until it reached the edge of the yard. From there the line was stretched across the road and for the width of our yard, it ran on the opposite side before returning to our property again.

"What happened, Grandpa?" David asked as he looked at the lines.

"Well, son," Daddy answered slowly in his southern drawl, "a man came out from the electric company and told me he'd have to cut off some big limbs of my oak trees. Told him he wasn't goin' to touch my trees, so they sent the foreman to talk to your Uncle Lewis since he now owns the farm. That man didn't get nowhere with him, neither. Lewis just pointed to me and said, 'You see that man? He's been livin' here a long, long time, and if he says you're not to cut on the trees, you just better not.' He then told the foreman, 'if you can't figure out another way to put in that line, then you better send someone out here who can!' You can see for yerself that someone did figure out a way to get the job done!"

And then David heard a remark that explained the whole episode. As my dad's eyes looked lovingly at the beautiful green symmetry of the ancient oaks he said softly, "Took God over a hundred years to grow them trees. Can't see ruining 'em for an electric line!"

Both Mama and Daddy lived over 90 years. During that time other trees, including the beautiful hickory tree that provided delicious large nuts with thin shells, grew old and the trunks rotted out. The trees were then cut down. Many trees, split down the middle by lightning, were scorched and died.

But the beautiful oaks remain.

CHARLIE'S VISITS

"You know how it is," Daddy said. "Every old crow thinks his is the blackest!"

His remark ruffled my feathers. His comment followed my assertion, "I think our baby is pretty special!"

I greeted my father with my new baby son in my arms, seeking his appreciation. Instead of admiring my child, he spoke of my sister's children. "Opal's kids are really somethin'. Just wait till you see her family." I wondered at my effort to please him.

I'll always remember that first trip carrying Charlie to the farm when he was three months old. Bill and I drove over 1600 miles from California in the dreaded heat and humidity. The trip, during the summer of 1951, proved miserable and terribly hot with no air conditioning. I breast-fed Charlie and he cried from colic and the heat. We finally arrived at the sweltering farmhouse, eager to show-off our first-born.

Bill's vacation time as a public school teacher fell during the stifling days of summer. Nevertheless, we returned year after year to visit the relatives, lugging our growing family.

In my memories I see my precious first-born on the farm: Charlie as a two-year-old eating watermelon, wearing only his skimpy white underpants; fishing for corncobs in Mama's washtub with a safety pin on a string tied to a bamboo pole; holding a cow's tail while my father milked by hand. Later as a teenager, he headed for the stock pond across the pasture with his younger sister tagging along, both carrying fishing poles.

Charlie had other special memories over the many years. One summer my Daddy gave him a baby calf to be sold at auction. He took Charlie, ten, and David, six, with him that day.

Daddy sat with Charlie on the raised bench seats looking down on the arena, while little David stood on his seat to get a better view. While Charlie and his grandpa kept an eye out for Charlie's calf, other animals were presented for auction. The auctioneer opened the bidding and searched the crowd to spot any bidding gestures. Daddy noticed David pointing as each animal was escorted in to be sold. Unaware of the workings of the auction and treating it more like a trip to the zoo, David's motions appeared to be bids on behalf of his grandfather. With a bit of a snicker, grandpa suggested to David that he might want to put down his hand unless he had money to pay for all the animals on which he was bidding.

Daddy gave my eldest son the $12.08 from the sale of the calf. My father acted less generously with his other grandchildren. Perhaps he felt a special kinship to Charlie, whose middle name, Arthur, was for him.

One year, Charlie and our youngest son, Bob, took their guitars on our trip and played and sang for a country musical at their cousin's house. My children loved the activities on the farm: fishing with the relatives, fish fries and hush puppies cooked in the big black wash pot, family reunions with loaded picnic tables and "all the cold soda pop you can drink."

Active in sports, music, and church activities, Charlie visited less and less after he entered high school and college.

When he enrolled in Washington University School of Dentistry in St. Louis, Missouri, he probably did not realize how incredibly homesick he might become. During the previous four years at Westmont College in Santa Barbara, California, he drove home on occasional weekends, holidays and special events.

It was too expensive to fly home to California from Missouri regularly. To ease the separation from his immediate family, he decided to visit his grandparents in nearby Arkansas.

My parents welcomed my son during the dental school years, urging him to come often. They showered him with attention and treasured the time together. My father introduced him in his own fashion as "My grandson, who is making a dentist."

In the farmhouse an honored guest asked the blessing aloud before eating. Meal after meal, Grandpa said, "Charlie, would you return thanks for our food?" Finally my son replied, "Grandpa, don't you think it's about time you took a turn?"

Although a city boy reared in comfort, my son adjusted well to rural life. He wrote that he enjoyed his grandmother's southern cooking. Charlie stood 6 feet 3 inches tall and Mama tried to "fatten him up," by baking pies and cakes. She sent him back to school with jelly and special treats.

In his letters home, our son described activities in the rural community. On one visit, Uncle Lewis took Charlie to town and asked him to choose a suit. My brother's generosity overwhelmed my son. He owned sport coats and pants, never before a suit. He attended the small white church with our relatives and entered into the activities at the farm.

The years sped by and my folks grew elderly and infirm. Charlie was unable to visit them at the farm, but he often mentioned that he would like to see his grandparents and other relatives.

In September of 1995, he made arrangements for a flight to Arkansas. Before Charlie made his reservations, he called Lewis and Gay to ask permission to stay at their house. Delighted, my brother immediately telephoned me in Oregon.

"You will never guess who's coming to visit!" Lewis exclaimed. "Would you believe Charlie plans to arrive here on my 58th birthday?"

The relatives welcomed him with hugs and kisses. The four days passed swiftly. During the final moments he went to say goodbye to his grandparents. Lewis told me later about the touching scene.

He said, "Oh, Sis, you would have been so proud of your son Charlie. He showed such great compassion and love and managed the sad parting unbelievably well."

As Charlie embraced my parents, he told them that someday he would meet them again in Heaven and prayed with them, while tears streamed down my parents' wrinkled cheeks. Both were in their nineties and suffered ill health. They probably knew they were saying a last goodbye to a beloved grandson.

Epilogue

Charlie did not see them again. Daddy died just 10 months after the visit, in July, 1996, and Mama two years later.

DADDY'S USEFUL HANDS

M y father, a man with a wide range of interests and capabilities, cherished his farm. He sang in the springtime as he plowed the soil for planting, while new green leaves decked the trees. He loved the changing of the seasons: long summer days with crops growing in the fields; harvest in the autumn with the leaves turning brilliant hues on the hillsides; cold winter days of hunting squirrel, ducks, geese, and rabbits to supplement the farm diet.

He did many things well: butchering hogs; sharpening tools, plows, and hoes; honing knives to a razor sharp edge on a whetstone; fashioning parts in the workshop for the farm machinery. I sometimes watched him cut bark from an elm tree for re-caning our straight-backed chairs. He prepared the bark by soaking it overnight in a tub of water. After removing the worn-out seat bottoms, he wove intricate designs to replace the old ones.

Daddy kept an "iron last" (shaped like a foot) for shoe repairs. He worked with his mouth full of tacks as he replaced soles. Carefully checking to see that no sharp nails were left to injure our feet, he then hammered the sole into place. Using a sharp knife, he trimmed around the edges to finish his handiwork.

He always kept his barbering tools handy to cut hair for anyone who asked. None of the kids had haircuts by a barber, and neither did most of the grown men. When he cut a young boy's hair for the first time Daddy asked, "Would you like a shave, too?" as he took out the shaving mug and lathered the brush. No one ever refused, and Dad pretended to shave the youngster after carefully lathering his face. In the middle of the procedure, he'd say, "Now open your mouth wide," and when the child automatically obeyed, Daddy swished the lathered brush in and out of the opened mouth.

Veterinarians were seldom consulted. Daddy doctored the animals using home remedies. He watched closely over cows having difficulty giving birth, literally pulling the new calves into the world. Desperate for additional cash during his younger years, Daddy trapped raccoons and opossums, skinning them and letting the skins dry on boards. He sold the pelts in town for a few extra nickels.

He wore patched overalls with a bib, heavy faded work shirts, and clodhopper farm shoes. When he went barefoot in the summer, the bottom of his feet became tough by walking in rocks, dirt, and stickers.

Daddy remained slim most of his life. He moved quickly and easily outworked others picking cotton, hauling hay, or milking cows. When chopping cotton, he reached the end of the rows first. His cotton sack filled more rapidly and weighed more than most; he mended fences, plowed crops, and shocked hay rapidly. He picked blackberries with both hands, filling his bucket before anyone else.

My father worked constantly, even in the wintertime, cutting trees for firewood and clearing the land for additional crops and pasture. Huge piles of brush were left to dry until the debris would burn easily.

One day my elderly father tossed an armful of rubbish into the blazing inferno and snagged the chain attached to his gold pocket watch. He realized too late that his prized possession had gone into the fire, and he could not retrieve it.

He used every available means to make the farm more productive: consulting with the Soil Conservation Agent for crop rotation, terracing the land, filling in gullies with rocks picked up from the plowed fields. He planted legumes to add more nitrogen to the soil: alfalfa, clover, and purple-hulled peas. Manure from the cows and other livestock enriched the soil, and in later years, the chicken houses provided fertilizer.

Advancing into his eighties and nineties, Daddy's body gradually betrayed him as his health and strength declined. The calloused hands no longer held the handlebars of a plow or stacked hay with a pitchfork. Instead, he clutched the steering wheel of an all-terrain vehicle, his beloved four-wheeler, as he slowly canvassed the well-worn paths of the farm, sometimes carrying a fishing pole to the nearest stream or pond.

On his final stay at the hospital, the journey completed, Daddy's hands fell idle, unmoving. When we were planning the clothes he should wear for his funeral, granddaughter Crystal exclaimed, "I know what I'd like Grandpa to wear. His bib overalls and work shirt!"

But Daddy always dressed up for special occasions, and this was to be his last big event on earth. We chose a nice sports jacket and matching pants, given to him by Lewis and Gay, and a brand-new white shirt purchased at Wal-Mart. I think he'd have been pleased at how "grand" he looked.

STRENGTH FOR EACH DAY

s I recall Mama throughout my growing-up years, I'm
amazed at her resilience as she faced the responsibilities of
daily living.

My father seemed a poor prospect as a husband and provider,
for he had only a fourth grade education, having little time for
school after his father committed suicide. Nevertheless, he worked
hard, determined to earn a living on the worn-out farm that
suffered from neglect.

Mama went to the fields to help with the backbreaking work.
Once when I complained about being tired, Mama replied, "Oh,
my, you don't even know what the word means!"

My mother came home at noon to prepare a simple meal, often
dried beans cooked earlier; cornbread baked in an iron skillet,
and potatoes fried in bacon drippings. As summer progressed, we
picked vegetables from our garden to augment the meager diet.
A large meal at noon fortified us for the long afternoon in the
fields. We ate supper that consisted mainly of leftover cornbread
crumbled in milk, eaten with a cold slice of ham or side pork.
When summer weather left the kitchen stifling, it was too hot to
cook on the wood stove.

In addition to the fieldwork and preparing meals, Mama
milked cows, slopped pigs, and fed chickens. She washed clothes
on a washboard and boiled the white clothing in a big iron kettle,
using soap made from a combination of grease and lye.

With a hand-pushed cultivator, my mother tilled the soil for her garden, planted seeds and picked vegetables. With a little help from her kids, she prepared vegetables for eating and cooking: washing, peeling, shelling the beans and peas. She broke green beans, pickled the cucumbers, and shucked corn. Working in a threadbare dress drenched with perspiration, Mama canned fruit and vegetables for the winter. She helped butcher hogs, cut up meat and grind sausage. She canned meat in glass jars using a pressure cooker.

When friends visited, Mama caught a chicken for the meal, using crumbs to lure the victim within reach. Holding the fowl on the chopping block with one hand, Mama cut off the head with the big axe. I've also seen her wring a chicken's neck and throw the flapping creature on the ground during its final moments. Before plucking the feathers, she dipped the chicken in boiling water and then removed the small fluff and pinfeathers by singeing over an open fire. Her sharp knife split the middle to remove the insides, deftly separating the liver, heart and gizzard for cooking. She'd hold the gizzard in one hand to cut open and remove the contents while showing us kids the small gravel debris inside. She rolled the pieces in flour seasoned with salt and pepper, and fried in a large black iron skillet filled almost to the top with grease.

From time to time the wrong chicken would be chosen for killing, for we would find a well-formed egg and many smaller ones, which meant that we had picked one of the "laying hens."

Life was not easy and tempers would flare, but I rarely heard her complain about her difficult life with no luxuries and few of what I consider necessities. She did complain about Daddy teasing her, as he did when she got a new cook stove. He told everyone about buying the stove and then added, "And dad-gum if Jewell didn't burn the biscuits the very first morning!" Mama always took the bait and responded in anger, "Now, Arthur, you know as well as I do, I did not let the biscuits burn!"

Mama spent a lot of time "mothering Daddy." She carried him glasses of cold water, laid his clothes out for him to wear, and served his plate first with his favorite foods. She gave him the most desirable parts of the fried chicken, while she ate the neck or back or gizzard. He received the best piece of cake, the biggest serving of banana pudding. She worried if he seemed overtired or ill. She constantly reminded us to "obey your daddy, hug your daddy, and take the popcorn to your daddy."

Her overwhelming need for sleep caused by narcolepsy may have contributed to weight gain during pregnancy, pounds she could never lose. At one time she weighed over three hundred pounds.

"Jewell, you've got to lose weight," her well-meaning friends told her. "You won't live very long carrying all those pounds around!" Mama got even; she outlived her contemporaries. She wished to lose the additional pounds and never could until illness near her 90th year reduced her to a frail old woman.

Perhaps because of hardships caused by the lack of money during the early years together, my folks were extremely frugal. Daddy controlled the finances. He bought the food, household items, clothing, and farm equipment and counted out the money, coin by coin and paid cash.

Mama often told her children she loved us. She did whatever she could to ease the pain of our poverty, but she was powerless to get Daddy to spend money for clothing, toys, or treats when we begged for them.

Year after year, Mama did what she considered necessary, rising before daybreak to prepare the farmhouse meals. I never once heard her say what she would have liked her life to be: hopes, goals, or her disappointments. She performed her daily tasks with whatever means she had, never wasting anything that could be used, either by her own family or the neighbors.

During her final years when she was thin, I packed some of my size twelve clothing and mailed to her. She was thrilled, telling me, "I've never had so many beautiful clothes in my life!" I found out later that she was reluctant to unpack the box for she wanted to share with her friends and family "how nice each piece of clothing was, and how neatly it had been packed."

Daddy loved my mother, but as far as I knew, he never once sent her flowers, cards, or gifts. He never acknowledged her birthday or their anniversary. I never saw him hug or kiss my mom or heard him compliment her. And yet near the end of their lives when Mama was hospitalized for tests for the anemia, he sat by her bedside, day after day, hour after hour, reluctant to leave her. There was never any doubt in my mind that Mama and Daddy had taken their marriage vows seriously, and that they were always true to each other.

For most of their lives together, Daddy appeared to have fewer health problems. During the three years my mother needed blood transfusions every two weeks, we did not think that she would outlive him. She fought a hard battle to stay alive for his sake.

On the night that he died, Mama had gone to bed and was asleep when my brother and I came from the hospital to tell her the sad news. I'll never forget the wailing cries when she was told that Daddy had died. I finally crawled into bed beside her and held her in my arms until she finally slept.

From that time on, and until her death two years later, Mama needed constant care. However, a mystery remains that no one has been able to solve. After Daddy's death her blood count returned to normal.

Thanks to Daddy's obsession to save money and invest in tax-free stocks and bonds, money was available to pay caregivers for Mama to finish her days on the farm; as she wished. A few days before her death, as I approached the house, I heard my mom and her caregiver singing *The Old Rugged Cross*. Mama was ready to meet the Savior who died on that cross.

Opportunity to Bless

M any years after I wrote about yearning for my father to speak the words, "I love you," I heard a similar lament from my younger brother. Lewis had approached our father when he realized Daddy would not live much longer. He begged, "Please, Dad, I need to hear you say the words. Please tell me to my face, 'I love you'." But Daddy refused to bless my brother with those three precious words.

The silence left Lewis hurt and confused. He told me, "I know Dad loves me, but I can't understand why he cannot tell me! Dadgumit, Sis, why is that so hard to do?"

His voice held such intense sadness I wished to hold him to soothe his pain, as I did when he was a little boy. Instead I could only say, "I wish I had an answer, but I do not know." I then shared what I had written about my own pain, years before; searching for the reason Daddy would not express his love for me in words I longed to hear.

When our father lay barely conscious in a hospital room, hooked up to the monitoring machines, Lewis took his wife, Gay, to visit one last time. Though my father was unresponsive, my brother told Daddy of his overwhelming love, of his appreciation for the life that consisted so much of work and self-denial. My brother spoke of the contributions Daddy made throughout the years, and how he had always been there for him. Gay later told me the intense emotion rushed out in a steady stream of sobs and tears.

She shared the agonizing scene. "I stood there and witnessed such an outpouring of love and devotion, holding my husband through it all. I did not dare let myself shed even one tear, for if I had lost control, I felt I would never stop crying."

There was no response from our father.

The following night I arrived, along with my husband and grown son David. We landed during a terrible rain and lightning storm, delaying our flight from Oregon. When we reached the hospital during the early morning hours, the nurses told us that Daddy would not know we were there. And yet, we felt he tried to talk to us.

I hugged and kissed my father, telling him who we were. I asked David to pray aloud for his grandfather. He thanked God for Grandpa and asked that God accept him into His loving arms. Then we noticed Daddy open his eyes and began moving his lips.

David said, "Grandpa, we think you recognize us and wish to tell us." Suddenly Daddy's hand touched David's arm. Possibly he knew we were coming and waited for our arrival.

My father died that same day.

In the midst of my loss, I became aware that the blessing I desired would never be spoken.

I learned many years before Daddy died that his actions demonstrated his love. Did I think that his failure to say the words meant he did not love me? Oh, no, I always knew, just as my younger brother said, "I know Dad loves me!"

Daddy was determined to provide for us against impossible odds: he was ill-equipped to do anything except farm, starting as a sharecropper without land, livestock, equipment or finances. He focused on accumulating and earning money. All those years, starting with the Depression and continuing throughout his life, he saved every penny, never allowing himself anything special.

If work could kill, my father would have died young. He rose in darkness before dawn and many times worked until after dark. I never heard him complain. He was so intent on providing essentials, he seemed to have no idea that his children had unmet emotional needs. For most of my life I held him accountable for not recognizing those needs, even though he said, "I did the very best I knew how."

After I became a parent, I realized I could never completely fulfill the expectations of my children, just as my father never fulfilled mine. Grasping that knowledge, I asked the Lord to grant me forgiveness and that He erase the long-standing sadness. As I accepted my own failures, I embraced the courage, dignity, and compassion taught by Daddy's life.

A dear friend said, "Remember, there are more ways to express love than saying the words." Each day I seek to accept that message and dwell on the character traits from my father that blessed my life.

I make the words of the beautiful hymn my goal, "Make Me a Blessing."

Out of my pain and frustration came a lesson that serves me well. My children and grandchildren will never need to ask if I love them. I speak the beautiful words aloud every chance I get.

"I love you!"

Glossary

andiron — The metal device in a fireplace that supports firewood, allowing air to circulate under the fire, and connected to an upright guard that keeps the burning wood in place.

battery radio — Since there was no electricity on the farm, the only news we heard that did not come by word of mouth was by battery radio. My dad learned of my brother's ship going down from a news bulletin on my Aunt Altie's radio.

bean flip — Homemade slingshot. Pieces of rubber inner tube were attached to a hand-held Y shaped tree branch and to a pocket crafted from an old tongue of a shoe shaped to hold a projectile.

bread & butter pickles — Sweet pickles made with sliced cucumbers.

briar stitch & hemstitch — Briar stitch is a fancy hand-embroidered stitch that appears in V shapes. Hemstitch or hem-stitch is a technique used to decorate pillowcases and dresser scarves.

bushel basket — Wooden slat basket, often used to measure a volume of peaches and apples. Smaller than a washtub, made of thin slats of wood, held about 1.25 cubic feet.

cash crop	Anything the farmers grew that was sold for cash. The money gained would be the only income we had to live on until the next year. As sharecroppers, our cash crop was cotton.
chiggers	Tiny, tiny bugs that seemed to burrow under a person's skin, and caused itching. We usually got them when picking blackberries or sitting on grass. Mother would always say, "rub yourself good with kerosene to keep the chiggers off," but it didn't work very well. The insects disappear during winter.
choppin' cotton	Thinning out the cotton plants in the springtime, spacing the plants by the width of a hoe, and removing the weeds and grass growing between the plants.
coming forward	Also known as "going forward." Leaving your place in the pew to move to the front of the church. Usually people came forward at the invitation of the preacher at revival meetings. People came forward for prayer and asking to be saved, or proclaiming their faith. A public affirmation of one's desire or decision to come to the Lord, to rededicate their life to serve the Lord.
cooties	Lice found in hair and often passed to others. School children's hair was examined for lice during outbreaks.

cotton	Cotton has to be planted every year. Field work never took place on Sunday, nor did any other non-essential farm work. Only essential work like milking cows and caring for livestock was performed on Sunday. It was usually very dry during the picking days. The long heavy canvas collection sack would drag behind you. The whole family picked, side-by-side with other families, white families working together with black families. Each person had their own sack that would be weighed and entered in the books with the name of the picker.
Cracklins	Pork rinds (pork skin), fried until very crisp, sometimes baked in cornbread batter.
Crayola	Brand name for colored wax crayons used for drawing. Crayola is often used interchangeably with the word crayon.
Dresser Scarves	Decorative piece of material placed on top of dressers or chests of drawers, sometimes trimmed in lace or embroidered.
flatiron	A very heavy appliance shaped like a modern clothes iron, but with metal handle and solid flat base. Heated on the top of the wood stove or in front of the fireplace, used to iron clothing. Almost everything was ironed (all made of cotton), sheets, pillowcases, table scarves, as well as clothing.
freshen	When the fresh milk "comes in" after a calf is born. "The cow has freshened" — cow has a new calf so the milk cycle starts again.

GI allotment checks	Amount given to those in military service after coming back from WWII. Often used for education, but could be used any way desired.
goose locks	Slang for the small fluffy left-over pieces of cotton that were passed over at the main harvest. Tiny bits of cotton left in the cotton boll (round seed capsule of cotton plants) after the picking was done. After frost and without green leaves, it was easy to see. Kids would go out and gather cotton in apron sacks.
go to the bottoms	Low lying areas of farms where the runoff from the rains and creeks deposited the richest top soil, providing the best land to grow cotton.
laid by	After the planting, growing, and weeding, when it was time to wait for the plants to produce, a time when plants are left undisturbed. Once "laid by," no longer plowed, chopped, or weeded. Crops were left to grow until the fall at harvesting.
Limoges china	Highly valued French china.
lock of cotton	Small bits of cotton left in the cotton boll after picking. Same as goose locks. Children were sent to pick the remaining cotton after harvest and placed in little bags tied around the waist.

long distance call	Telephone calls made to persons outside of local call zone incurred additional expense and added to a monthly phone bill, only used when absolutely necessary, considered a great extravagance. Typical calls were kept under 3 minutes and rushed due to cost.
long handled underwear	Winter underwear. The farmers put them on at the start of the cold weather and sometimes worn all winter without changing. A one piece white garment with long sleeves and long pants.
lye soap	Soap made by combining the fat from hogs with purchased can of lye. Cooked until all scraps dissolved, it congealed into soap. Some families made their own lye by dripping water through ashes.
mince meat	Mixture of chopped dried fruit, spices and sometimes chopped meat; beef or venison.
mourner's bench	The Baptist church placed a wooden bench at the front of the church, just down from the pulpit, for people to come and pray, to seek the Lord. Many times people were saved on the mourner's bench. During the service a person might walk to it and sit down praying. Sometimes others would join them in support and pray with them.
party line	A telephone connection where multiple households share the line (party line) and anyone has the ability to listen in on the conversation of others.
poke sack	Any kind of sack that will hold items, usually made of paper.

right hand of fellowship	A welcoming handshake of partnership and brotherhood extended to new members of a congregation, roots of the practice found in Galatians 2:9.
rural mail delivery	The U.S. postal service daily delivery (by car), Monday through Saturday, to the mailboxes next to the road.
sharecroppers shack	A small two room building, one room for sleeping and sitting and the other for cooking, owned by the landowner. The Sharecropper was allowed to stay while working the land. Often the roof leaked and the boards that formed the walls were spaced so far apart that newspaper was used to try to keep out the wind and cold. The floor was made of boards. There was no bathroom, indoor plumbing, electricity, phone, or gasoline operated equipment. An outhouse and well were nearby. There was never any opportunity for the Sharecropper to own the shack and there was no rent payment required.
snuff glasses	Snuff (powdered tobacco) was sold in 4" glass containers, later used as drinking glasses.
souse meat	Meat from boiled hog's head and ears, spices added and then mashed fine.
spit bath	Use of a washcloth wet with soap and water to wash the body. No bathroom or shower or any place private to bathe. Washtubs were occasionally used as improvised bathtubs.

stock pond	A pond for the livestock to drink from. Most were filled by rain water and would go dry in the summer. Some were filled by springs.
sweat bees	Little bees stung people when wet with perspiration.
scrappin cotton	Small amounts of cotton left on the ground or in the boll. Even though it brought only a few pennies more, it was worth collecting.
strip down cows bag	Getting the last amount of milk out of the cow's bag, stripping the last amount out of the bag.
survival furlough	During World War II, service members in disasters, such as ships sinking or units with great loss of life, were given time off to go home and then return to duty.
telegram	A communication used to advise of timely matters, a death in the family, congratulations, birthday greetings, arrivals. Working for Western Union, at our small office, we wore headsets to take phone calls while transcribing the caller's words. We then read the message back to the caller. After the message was sent to the destination office by teletype, it was printed and delivered by carrier or U.S. mail. The caller indicated how the message was to be paid for. At times we contacted the recipient of a telegram by phone and read it to them.

tow sack	We referred to burlap sacks as tow sacks, though I've later found there is strong opinion that tow sacks are made of flax or hemp. Our "tow sacks" were burlap. To make a swing, we would fill a tow sack with straw, tie it to a cable hung on a limb of the large oak tree, and swing back and forth.
trace chain	The chain that goes from the wagon or plow to the horse's harness that bears most of the pulling strain.
Victrola	A wind up record player often referred to by the company name, "Victrola."
weed stickers	Any weeds with thorny protrusions, sometimes nettles, stabbing bare legs, feet, and clothing.

Events Timeline

Daddy's birth	March 2, 1904
Mama's birth	November 29, 1905
Hershel's birth	December, 1925
Loretta's birth	August, 1927
Opal's birth	August, 1929
Great Depression starts	October, 1929
WPA created	April, 1935
Lewis' birth	September, 1937
Saved & Baptized	Summer, 1938
Great Depression ends	1939-1941
Pearl Harbor attack	December 7, 1941
Sinking of the Bismarck Sea	February 21, 1945
Germany surrenders	May 7, 1945
High School graduation	June, 1945
Left farm to Little Rock	June, 1945
Western Union job	July, 1945
Japan surrenders-End of WWII	August, 1945
Transferred to California	December, 1945
Married William Mehl	September 11, 1948
Children born	1951, 1954, 1959, 1961
Daddy's death	July 23, 1996
Mama's death	May 17, 1998

Printed in the United States
By Bookmasters